27 MAR 2018

new Ideas in
Ribboncraft

new Ideas in
Ribboncraft

Susan Niner Janes

NORTH LIGHT BOOKS
CINCINNATI, OHIO

www.artistnetwork.com

dedication

For my parents, Belle and Robert Niner. Heartfelt thanks for encouraging

me to pursue my creative ambitions. I love you both.

New Ideas in Ribboncraft. © 2003 by Susan Niner Janes. Manufactured in China [Singapore]. All rights reserved. The patterns and drawings in the book are for personal use of reader. By permission of the author and publisher, they may be either hand-traced or photocopied to make single copies, but under no circumstances may they be resold or republished. It is permissible for the purchaser to make the projects contained herein and sell them at fairs, bazaars and craft shows. No other part of this book may be reproduced in any form or by any electronic or mechanical means including information storage and retrieval systems without permission in writing from the publisher, expect by a reviewer, who may quote a brief passage in review. Published by North Light Books, an imprint of F&W Publications, Inc., 4700 East Galbraith Road, Cincinnati, Ohio 45236. (800) 289-0963. First edition.

07 06 05 04 03   5 4 3 2 1

Library of Congress Cataloging-in-Publication Data

Janes, Susan Niner

    New ideas in ribboncraft/ by Susan Niner Janes

        p. cm.

        ISBN 1-58180-351-6 (alk. paper)

        1. Ribbon work. I. Title.

TT850.5 J36 2003

745.4'4--dc21

                    2002038002

Editor: Catherine Cochran and Tricia Waddell
Designer: Andrea Short
Production Artist: Karla Baker
Production Coordinator: Michelle Ruberg
Photographers: Christine Polomsky, Tim Grondin and Al Parrish
Photo Stylist: Jan Nickum

metric conversion chart

TO CONVERT	TO	MULTIPLY BY
Inches	Centimeters	2.54
Centimeters	Inches	0.4
Feet	Centimeters	30.5
Centimeters	Feet	0.03
Yards	Meters	0.9
Meters	Yards	1.1
Sq. Inches	Sq. Centimeters	6.45
Sq. Centimeters	Sq. Inches	0.16
Sq. Feet	Sq. Meters	0.09
Sq. Meters	Sq. Feet	10.8
Sq. Yards	Sq. Meters	0.8
Sq. Meters	Sq. Yards	1.2
Pounds	Kilograms	0.45
Kilograms	Pounds	2.2
Ounces	Grams	28.4
Grams	Ounces	0.04

about the author

Susan Niner Janes is an American craft designer, author and editor living in England. She writes for adults and children on subjects ranging from fabric crafts and sewing to papercrafts, printing and rubber stamping. This is her seventh craft book. She is also a frequent contributor of projects for craft magazines. Her work has been featured in publications such as *Crafts Beautiful*, *Arts & Crafts* and *Prima*. Before moving to England, Susan was the assistant needlework and crafts editor for *Woman's World* magazine. As a Certified Professional Demonstrator, Susan creates sample projects for craft manufacturers and demonstrates crafts at consumer shows. She holds a degree in apparel design from Cornell University.

acknowledgments

Thanks to my loving, supportive, and good-natured family, Leah, Daniel and husband, Michael, who put up with mountains of creative clutter and a frequent diet of micro meals. You're great!

A big thank-you to the inspirational North Light team, and especially editors Catherine Cochran and Tricia Waddell, for being consummate professionals, always insightful and helpful.

Hats off to North Light Books for producing the books crafters dream about and for making this craft author's dreams come true.

table of contents

it's a ribbon wonderland

ibbon is one of life's affordable luxuries—a little touch of something elegant that turns the everyday into the exception.

Ribbon and special occasions go hand in hand—an oversized bow on a birthday gift, the delicate streamers trailing from a bride's bouquet, a blue-ribbon prize. A ribbon is just a narrow band of fabric, but it is nearly always made of something special, whether it is shimmering satin, gossamer taffeta or luxurious velvet. These special fabrics mark special times, and it only takes a small bow to make a noticeable difference.

One of the most exciting things about ribboncraft is the amazing variety of ribbons available. Your local craft store is a ribbon wonderland! So many different widths, fabrics and textures to choose from: satin, sheers, grosgrain, velvet, jacquard, wire-edge, rat-tail cord, ready-made ribbon rosebuds. Ribboncraft encompasses an amazing spectrum of activities from weaving and embroidery, to lacing and flower-making. Ribbons can dress up garments, decorate home furnishings, make greeting cards unique and transform gifts into treasured keepsakes.

So, what can you expect to find in this book? Something for everyone, whether you are a skilled crafter or an eager beginner. You'll find three chapters: Home Accents shows you ways to decorate towels, placemats and lampshades; Gifts and Keepsakes includes a Snowflake Holiday Stocking and a Beaded Penny Rug Purse; and Wedding and Baby is filled with projects to commemorate the two most exciting events of your life.

Remember, the ribboncrafts you produce help to make special days more memorable. And the pleasure of crafting with ribbon can make an ordinary day special. Pretty good for a narrow band of fabric....

Happy Ribboncrafting!
—Susan Niner Janes

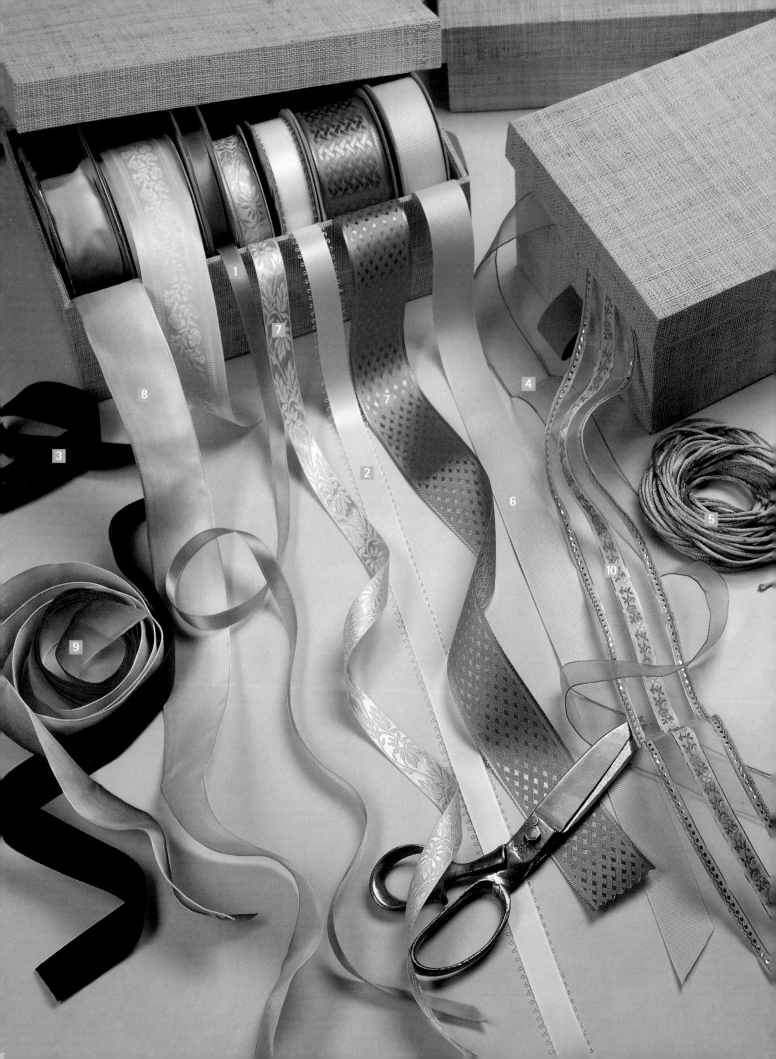

The ribbons used in this book are woven-edge ribbons or narrow bands of fabric with selvages—tightly woven edges that prevent unraveling—on both sides. Because the edges are finished, woven-edge ribbons can be washed repeatedly and are therefore suitable for long-lasting craft projects, such as clothing or home accents.

Here is a list of the most commonly used ribbons that you will use for the projects in this book.

all about ribbon

1 Satin

Nothing can compare to the lustrous sheen and texture of satin ribbon. The good news is that it's also easy to care for since polyester satin can be machine-washed and dried, and usually requires no ironing. Many of the projects in this book use satin ribbon, which comes in an amazing range of widths and colors, making it suitable for all sorts of projects, from ribbon embroidery to gathered flowers.

There are two types of satin ribbon: single-face satin, which has one lustrous and one matte surface; and double-face satin, which is lustrous on both sides. When should you use each? If you are tying a bow, choose double-face satin, since both sides of the ribbon will show. Double-face satin is thicker, so it is more suitable for glued projects (the glue is less likely to seep through). Single-face satin is ideal for stitched trims in which only the top side of the ribbon shows. Single-face satin is also slightly less expensive, so to save money, use it whenever possible.

2 Feather-Edge

Also known as picot-edge, this satin ribbon has wispy loops along its edges. Use it on trims for feminine projects, such as sachets.

3 Velvet

Velvet ribbons have a luxurious pile finish, which makes them weighty. Nylon velvet is washable and crease-resistant. Velvet ribbon is stunning during autumn and winter, especially for the holidays, because of its deep, rich colors.

4 Sheer

Translucent ribbons, such as organdy, are perfect for romantic, whimsical effects. Some sheer ribbons, such as the ones used in the wedding projects, combine satin stripes with the sheer effect.

5 Rat-Tail

Not quite ribbon because it isn't flat, rat-tail cord is very useful and attractive, despite its name. This silky cord is often used for beading. It comes in handy when making drawstrings and bag straps. Also, rat-tail cord is often braided or used when making tassels.

6 Grosgrain

Grosgrain is a strong, tightly woven ribbon recognizable by its narrow cross-wise ridges.

7 Jacquard and Brocade

Jacquard ribbon has woven patterns, and brocades are jacquards with raised patterns. Multi-colored jacquards have an embroidered look.

8 Taffeta

Taffeta is a crisp, tightly woven ribbon, available in solids, plaid and moiré effects. It makes great bows that retain their shape well.

9 Wire-Edge Ribbon

This ribbon has narrow wires woven into its selvages. The wires are flexible so the ribbon can be bent into formations that hold their shape, such as a ribbon rose (see page 26) or large bows.

10 Novelty Ribbons

This is a catch-all category to cover the staggering array of specialty ribbons that are available. Novelty ribbons include metallics, printed ribbons, gingham checks and plaids.

Ribboncraft is so versatile because you can use it in many different types of craft projects and pair it with many types of materials. This makes for very dynamic, creative projects, but it also means that you'll have to stock up on other craft materials such as papercraft and sewing supplies. The small investment is well worth it, however, because the results are so rewarding!

materials & supplies

✳ ADHESIVES

Keep the following adhesives, sealants and protectants on hand when creating your unique ribbon projects. Not only are they necessary for constructing the project, but they also seal the ends of ribbons to prevent fraying.

Craft Glue

Craft glue is handy for sealing ribbon ends and gluing non-washable ribboncraft projects, especially those involving paper. It dries clear and flexible.

Clear Nail Polish

Although this is not an adhesive, it is a quick-drying sealant for ribbon ends. Be careful—it is flammable, so do not use it for projects you will place near a heat source.

Fabric Glue

Use fabric glue to seal ribbon ends on washable projects, and for gluing ribbon to fabric. You can find this at your local craft or fabric store.

Liquid Seam Sealant

A liquid seam sealant, such as Fray Check, seals ribbon ends so they won't unravel. It is available at your local fabric store.

Glue Stick

A glue stick is very useful when working with paper punches and other paper-based decorative embellishments that you can add to your ribboncraft projects.

Fusible Web

Fusible web is an iron-on adhesive that permanently bonds two layers of fabric together. It comes on a paper backing and is very easy to use. You can find it in craft and fabric stores.

Masking Tape

Masking tape is indispensable for attaching templates to project surfaces.

Adhesives seal ribbons and prevent fraying, keeping your projects clean and finished.

SHOPPING ADVICE:

Fabric stores stock woven-edge ribbons and paper stores stock craft ribbons, but hobby superstores carry both. Craft ribbons, also known as cut-edge ribbons, are stiffened strips of fabric, plastic or paper with unfinished edges. They are used by florists and for gift wrapping—projects for temporary use. Do not purchase them by mistake. Make sure that you are buying the right stuff!

You can find a wide assortment of decorative papers as well as embellishments like paper punches, hole punches and pre-cut designs at your local craft store.

✳ PAPER

Several different types of paper are used in this book. Check out your local art, scrapbooking or paper supply store to see the wide variety of papers available for craft projects.

Corrugated Cardboard

Corrugated cardboard has fluted ridges that make it very flexible. It comes in several colors and is excellent for use in paper ribboncrafts because it is sturdy and durable.

Cardstock

Cardstock is another very strong surface to use for paper ribboncrafts. It is widely available in a multitude of colors at your local craft store.

Handmade Paper and Giftwrap

Giftwrap is soft and supple, and is suitable for covering boxes. Use hand-made papers with visible fibers for added texture.

Pearlescent Paper

Papers with pearly or iridescent finishes are a recent trend in crafts. They are available in a wide range of colors and are ideal for festive occasions.

Vellum

Vellum comes in a large selection of colors and weights. It is ideal for lampshades or mobiles.

✳ PAPER TOOLS

Paper punches are a great way to add a simple decorative touch to your ribboncraft projects. They are available in a multitude of sizes and shapes, suiting your own personal style. These items can be found at your local craft or scrapbooking store.

Hand Punches

Hand punches enable you to make uniformly sized holes quickly, and are suitable for use on either paper or felt. The 1/16" (1.6mm) circle punch is used extensively in this book to punch holes for ribbon lacing. Other useful sizes are the 1/8" (3mm) circle and the 1/4" (7mm) circle.

Paper Punches

These punches are inexpensive and add a polished finish to your paper ribboncrafts. Press-down punches are available in a wide range of die-cut shapes. For this book, you will need small and large heart punches, and a large flower-shaped punch.

Metal Ruler

Use rulers when cutting or scoring paper, as well as for measuring.

Craft Knife and Cutting Mat

Use a craft knife for cutting and scoring paper and cardboard. It will give you accurate, professional results. Use a self-healing cutting mat whenever you use a craft knife.

✳ SCISSORS

All the scissors that you'll need for this book are listed in this section. Remember to keep papercraft scissors for paper use and sewing scissors for fabric use. Never mix them up—you'll dull the blades!

Nail Scissors

Whether you choose straight or curved nail scissors is your own preference. They are indispensible for crafts and ideal for fine cutting. Keep a pair expressly for papercraft projects.

Paper Edgers

Paper edgers are like pinking shears, but are made expressly for papercraft use. A variety of decorative blade patterns are available fairly inexpensively, so collecting them can become an obsession. For this book, I used Fiskars Clouds, Scallop and Wave paper edger patterns.

Needlecraft Scissors

These scissors are about 5" (12cm) long, a handy size for ribboncraft projects. The pointed blades are ideal for snipping threads and angling ribbons. They are also used to cut felt or fabric.

Pinking Shears

Use pinking shears for cutting patterned edges on fabrics, such as tulle or felt. They are longer and heavier than paper edgers. Pinking shears are now available with scalloped blades, in addition to the traditional zigzag pattern.

❋ SEWING SUPPLIES

Even if you have never tried to sew before, you will learn how simple ribboncraft projects can be. Here are some sewing supplies that you should have available before starting any of the projects in this book.

Iron-On Interfacing

Use iron-on interfacing to strengthen and stabilize fabrics and prevent puckering. Interfacing is available in fabric stores.

Machine-Washable Felt

Felt is a fabric made from fibers that have been compressed and tangled to produce a soft, fuzzy surface. The advantage of felt over other fabrics is that its edges, when cut, will not fray, and require no finishing. This is a great timesaver, especially for beginners. In the past, felt could not be washed, so it was used for cheap and cheerful cut-and-glue crafts. Today, machine-washable felt is available in a wide assortment of colors and styles, and will give your projects a longer lifespan. I used Kunin Rainbow Classic Felt for the projects in this book.

Iron

Keep an iron and ironing board handy when you begin working on fabric ribboncrafts. Not only will you want to press your ribbons and fabrics for a crisp, finished project, but you will need the heat from an iron to bond interfacing and fusible web.

Needles

For this book, you will need both sewing needles and embroidery needles. The embroidery needles required are a chenille needle (large eye, pointy tip) and a tapestry needle (large eye, blunt tip). Embroidery needles are used for ribbon embroidery and must be large enough to accommodate a $1/8$" (3mm) wide ribbon. You may also use a tapestry needle when piercing holes in paper ribboncraft projects.

Straight Pins

Straight pins are suitable for most sewing projects. Use them for temporarily holding fabrics together during the construction process.

HAND-SEWING VS. USING A SEWING MACHINE:

The projects in this book use basic sewing techniques that you can easily learn. For some of the projects, this is a basic hand-stitch. For other projects, light use of a sewing machine is recommended. All of the projects that I suggest you use a sewing machine for are clearly marked at the beginning of the instructions. The sewing machine work is a very simple, straight stitch, but should you choose not to use a machine, you may hand-stitch those steps as well.

Basic sewing supplies are all you need to easily create a decorative finish to your ribboncraft projects.

Silk Pins

Use silk pins when working with delicate fabrics like satin and sheers because they will not mark the fabrics. You will need to use them for the wedding projects in this book.

Tape Measure

Use a fabric tape measure to measure lengths of ribbon and fabric. They are usually available in 60" (150cm) lengths.

✳ SEWING NOTIONS AND EMBELLISHMENTS

A well-chosen finishing touch can transform a nice ribboncraft project into a breathtaking one. Buttons, beads, pearl beading, charms, machine-embroidered appliqués and ribbon roses add texture, color and shape to your projects. Remember, an embellishment should contribute to, but not overpower, a project.

Buttons

Add a sweet touch to a project by attaching a button with $1/8$" (3mm) ribbon. Look for buttons in novelty shapes and interesting textures.

Beads

You can find frosted, glass, plastic and semi-precious stone beads. They are available in a multitude of sizes and shapes. Also try using beads in graduated sizes.

Charms

Charms come in themed shapes (for example, baby motifs) and various metallic finishes. They are sewn onto projects through the top loops. Try sewing them on with ribbon, then tie a bow.

Pearl Beading

Pearl beading is available by the yard. To sew a cascading string of pearls onto your project, just catch the beads onto the background fabric with a few strategically placed stitches.

Machine-Embroidered Appliqués

Using ready-made embroidery is a real time-saver. Look for dainty florals because they look great with satin ribbon.

Ribbon Roses

Pre-formed ribbon roses are sold either individually or in packs. They are a great time-saver whenever a large quantity of roses is required.

How To Use The Patterns In This Book:

Project patterns are given whenever necessary in this book. You will have to enlarge most of them using a photocopier. Then transfer the pattern onto tracing paper, and finally onto your project. Applying self-adhesive plastic, such as clear Contact paper, makes the pattern durable and suitable for repeated use.

"Impressing" the design with a stylus (or a dry fine-point pen) is an easy way to transfer the design onto the surface of the project, leaving no pencil marks to erase. Use masking tape to secure the pattern in place.

When making a large quantity of one project, it is helpful to make templates of the pattern on heavy cardstock or poster board and cut them out with a craft knife.

Crafting with ribbons is easy to do, but there are a few tips and techniques that will help you to achieve

top-notch results every time. Note also that the ribbons used in this book are woven ribbons—not nonwoven

craft ribbons—and the techniques shown apply specifically to them. You'll also need to be familiar with a few

basic sewing techniques—these begin on page 18.

basic techniques

[RIBBON TECHNIQUES]

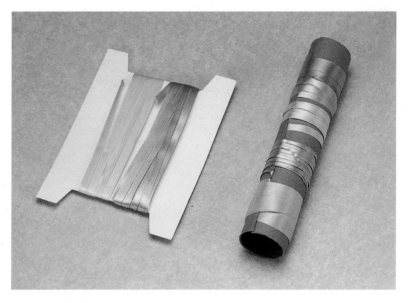

✳ STORING RIBBON

Many crafters are packrats, and who can blame them? After all, you never know just when you might need that beautiful piece of ribbon for a last-minute gift. Unfortunately, ribbon scraps can accumulate into a tangled mess. The image at the right shows a few suggestions for ribbon storage.

One option (LEFT) is to cut U-shaped notches in either side of cardboard, then wind ribbon around it. Cut vertical slits to catch the ribbon ends securely. Ribbon stored this way packs flat, but may require ironing when you use it.

The second storage idea (RIGHT) is to use a cardboard tube. Slit the tube lengthwise, then tuck the ribbon tails into the slit. Ribbon kept in this way requires no ironing when it is unwound. Empty thread spools and ribbon bolts are also excellent ways to store ribbon.

✳ CUTTING AND FINISHING RIBBON EDGES

It is important to carefully finish the ribbons that you cut to prevent frayed edges and unraveling projects! While this may seem like an unnecessary step, your projects will look neater and last longer if you follow these simple guidelines.

Cutting Ribbon Edges

Ribbon tails should always be neatly cut, whether straight or on the diagonal. Use this method for ensuring crisp edges every time.

Finishing Ribbon Edges

Scruffy-looking frayed ribbon tails can ruin the look of a fabulous project. To eliminate this problem, seal ribbon ends with craft glue.

Cut against a piece of masking tape. You can position the tape at exactly the angle you want. The tape edge provides a straight cutting guide.

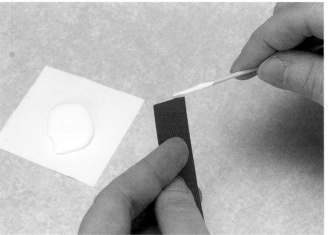

Apply the glue to the edges in a thin line. The glue dries clear and is non-toxic. Use for non-washable projects. Ribbon ends can also be sealed with clear nail polish. Ribbons sealed with nail polish are machine-washable. Nail polish, however, is flammable, so never use it on projects that will be placed near a heat source. The best choice for washable ribbon projects is to purchase a liquid seam sealant, such as Fray Check, to prevent unraveling.

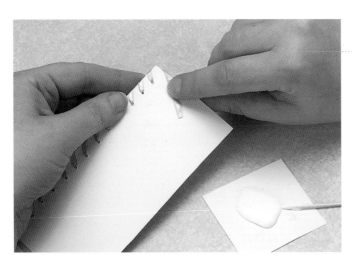

Glue down the ends on the back side of your work. You do not have to tie knots; plus the glue dries leaving a smooth finish to your work.

Finishing Ribbon Papercrafts

Ribbon papercrafts are simple to finish because you do not have to knot and tie them off, as with ribbon fabric crafts.

[SEWING TECHNIQUES]

✳ KNOT-FREE SEWING

Making a thread loop is a handy way to cut down on the number of knots in your sewing, since knots can look lumpy and messy.

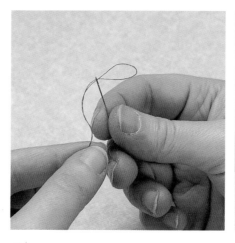

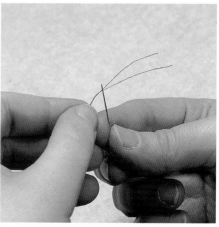

1 | *Fold thread in half, making a loop. Thread the loop and make a small stitch through fabric. Remove the needle from the loop.*

2 | *Bring the thread tails through the loop and pull tight. Then re-thread the needle with the tails. Continue sewing as normal.*

✳ TAILOR'S TACKS

Short thread loops are called tailor's tacks, and are used as a method of marking fabric without chalk or carbon paper (see Rose Garland Makeup Bag, page 96).

✳ BASTING

Basting is a way to sew two fabrics together temporarily until you can join them in a more permanent way. Basting is more precise than pinning.

✳ TACKING

Tacking is another simple stitch, connecting two pieces together. Often, you will tack ribbons together, tack ribbons and fabric together, or reinforce a bow by tacking it with a stitch.

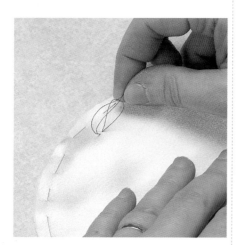

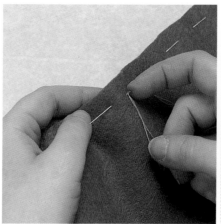

To make tailor's tacks, fold your thread in half and thread the loop end in your needle. Make a stitch through the fabric, then pull the tails through the loop and trim.

To baste two fabrics together, sew a widely spaced running stitch (in and out, repeat) through the fabrics you are joining. Remove the basting after the sewing has been completed.

Tacking is a simple technique, accomplished by making small stitches about the same length, very close together. Thread your needle, make the stitches and tie off with a knot on the back side of your project.

❋ FISH LOOP

A fish loop is a simple way of making a hanging loop out of ribbon. This can be used as a decorative hook to hang your project, as in the Snowflake Holiday Stocking, on page 78. Why is this called a fish loop? Just view the loop sideways!

Simply loop a piece of ribbon by crossing its tails, pin the cross-point and stitch it in place. Be sure to pin the ribbon flat; do not twist the ribbon and pin opposite sides together.

❋ RIBBON FRINGE

Adding fringe to your project is a quick and simple technique, but it really adds to the overall appeal. You can create this polished look by using ⅛" (3mm) wide satin ribbon that matches the colors in your project.

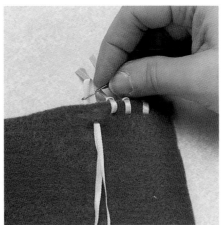

1 | *To make a decorative fringe, start with a piece of ⅛" (3mm) narrow ribbon, about 8" to 10" long (20cm to 25cm). Fold the ribbon in half to form a loop and thread the loop through the eye of an embroidery needle.*

2 | *Pass the ribbon tails through the loop and pull tight. You've now made one fringe loop. Repeat the process if you'd like more.*

You will definitely want to familiarize yourself with the stitches in this glossary. They are all simple embroidery stitches, easy to learn and execute. In no time, you will be creating fabulous ribboncraft projects!

stitch glossary

RIBBON EMBROIDERY

Satin ribbon is a natural for embroidery, but working with ribbon is slightly different from working with thread. First of all, it is best to keep your stitching simple, so that you can best appreciate the smooth satin surface and luster of the ribbon. Remember to keep the ribbon flat and untwisted as you stitch, and examine each stitch as you go.

You will need a needle with an eye large enough to fit the width of the ribbon. A chenille needle is used for stitching tightly woven fabrics, while a tapestry needle is suitable for loosely woven fabrics, or when stitching through prepunched holes (such as on the Granny Patchwork Pillow on page 42).

✳ CROSS STITCH

This familiar X-shaped stitch can be used to make decorative borders, or to fill in large areas. To make the stitch efficiently, sew a line of diagonals and then back-track in the other direction to complete the X.

 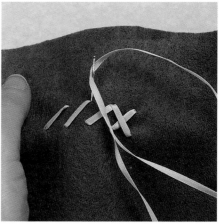

1 **Sew a row of diagonal stitches.**
Working from left to right, sew equally spaced diagonal lines. Stitch from lower left to top right, bringing the needle down vertically, as shown.

2 **Back-track to complete the Xs**
When you reach the end of the row, double back and sew the diagonal stitches from lower right to top left, as shown. Use the same holes as the first row of diagonals.

✳ BACK STITCH

This stitch is used for outlining. Back stitches are excellent for adding borders, lettering or creating pattern designs.

Bring the needle up a short distance from the previous stitch. Bring the needle down, in the hole of the previous stitch. Repeat these steps until you have completed your outlining.

✳ SLIP STITCH

This stitch is an almost-invisible way to join two fabrics together. Great for hems and appliqués—whenever a folded edge is present!

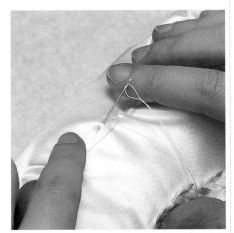

Bring the needle up through the folded edge. Catch a thread from the backing fabric. Re-insert the needle into the fold, and slide it along. Bring the needle out, pull the thread taut, and then repeat the catch-and-slide sequence.

✳ BLANKET STITCH

A blanket stitch is a decorative method of finishing an edge. As you might guess, woolen blankets are often finished in this way. A blanket stitch is a widely spaced version of a buttonhole stitch.

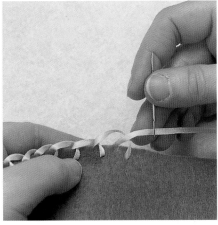

Bring the needle through the loop, then down into the fabric, a little away from the edge of the fabric. Bring the needle through the loop just formed. Repeat the cycle.

✳ BEADED BLANKET STITCH

Beaded borders are ideal in situations where weight is desired—such as tablecloth borders.

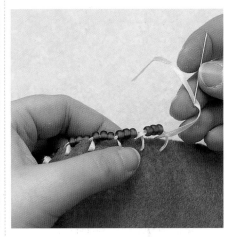

Bring the needle through the loop. Thread the beads onto the needle and slide them onto the ribbon. Put the needle through the edge of the fabric and repeat.

✳ FRENCH KNOT

This stitch creates a decorative knot that is ideal for flower centers. It gives your work dimension and texture.

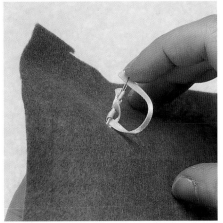

1 | *Bring a piece of threaded ribbon about 10" (25cm) long up through the fabric. Spiral the ribbon around the needle five times. Push the needle back down through the fabric and pull taut.*

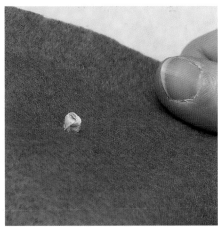

2 | *The finished knot forms a ball on the right side of the fabric. Tie the ribbon ends together on the wrong side of the fabric. Trim the ends close to the knot.*

Most often associated with prize-giving, a pin-on rosette bow can add decorative emphasis to all sorts of home

furnishings. To make a rosette, ribbon loops are arranged in a fan-like circular formation and stitched onto a

felt base. Two types of rosettes are shown. The flat-looped style is more tailored and sedate than the dramatic

petal-looped rosette. Try making both types. You can easily change the styles to suit your mood or the occasion.

decorative bows

1 Flat-Looped Rosette Bow

Ribbon

- 2¹/₂ yards (2.3m) of ⁷/₈" (23mm) wide single- or double-face satin ribbon
- 2 yards (2m) of 1¹/₂" (39mm) wide double-face satin ribbon

Supplies

- one 9" x 12" (23cm x 31cm) rectangle of machine-washable felt
- fusible web
- large decorative button
- needle and thread
- straight pins
- safety pin
- craft glue
- tape measure
- iron

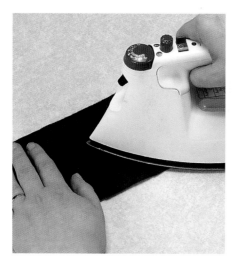

1 Make the Rosette Base

The rosette requires a thick base because it must support many layers of ribbon. Cut two small pieces of felt and sandwich fusible web in between. Bond the felt together following manufacturer's instructions. Cut a felt circle with a 3" (8cm) diameter for the base.

2 Add the Ribbon Loop

Mark the center of the circle with a piece of thread. Cut eighteen 4" (10cm) pieces of ⁷/₈" (23mm) ribbon for the rosette spiral. Seal the ribbon ends with glue. Finger-press (flatten or "press" with your finger or fingernail) the first piece of ribbon in half and pin the loop onto the felt. Using doubled sewing thread, catch the corner of the loop to the felt.

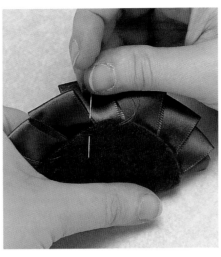

3 | Continue Adding Loops

Pin the ribbon loops onto the felt, angling and overlapping them as shown. Pin them in a clockwise spiral, until the circle is complete. Tuck the last loop under the first. Stitch a circle around the ribbon at the center of the rosette, through all layers.

4 | Stitch the Loops to the Felt

Using doubled sewing thread, sew around the wrong side of the rosette, catching each ribbon loop to the base. Make sure the stitching does not show on the front of the rosette.

5 | Sew a Button in the Center

Stitch a decorative shank-style button onto the rosette center using doubled sewing thread.

6 | Secure the Backing

Cut an 18" (45cm) piece of ⅞" (23mm) ribbon for the tail. Fold it in half and flatten the loop end into a V-point. Sew the point down. Trim the tail ends diagonally and seal them with glue. Sew the tail onto the rosette back. Sew a safety pin onto the rosette back. Make sure you stitch down the non-opening side of the safety pin.

You can easily pin this decorative bow to anything from a curtain tieback to a very special gift.

2 Petal-Looped Rosette Bow

Ribbon

- 2¼ yard (2.1m) of ⅝" (15mm) wide double-face satin ribbon
- 1¼ yard (1.2m) of ½" (12mm) wide metallic nylon taffeta ribbon

Supplies

- one 9" x 12" (23cm x 31cm) rectangle of machine-washable felt
- fusible web
- faux jewel button
- needle and thread
- straight pins
- safety pin
- craft glue
- tape measure
- iron

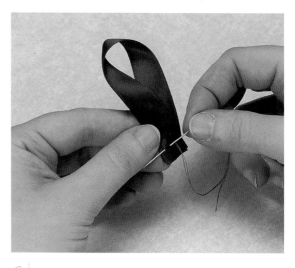

1 Make the Petal Loops

Cut fourteen 5½" (16cm) strips of satin ribbon. Seal the ends with craft glue. Fold each strip in half, then slide the left end over the right. Stitch the base of the loop together.

2 Add the First Loop

Cut two 3" (8cm) felt circles and join them to make a felt base with fusible web (see Flat-Looped Rosette Bow, step 1, page 22). Pin, then stitch, the first loop onto the base, sewing the left-hand corner.

3 Add the Loops Onto the Base

Pin, then stitch, the loops onto the base in a circular fashion.

4 Secure the Loops

On the back of the rosette, catch each ribbon loop to the base, using doubled sewing thread.

5 **Add Smaller Loops**

*Cut fourteen 3" (8cm) strips of metallic taffeta ribbon.
Seal the ends and make petal loops, just like you did in
step 1. Pin and stitch the loops, forming a smaller circle.*

6 **Sew a Button in the Center**

*Using doubled sewing thread, stitch the button onto
the center of the rosette.*

7 **Secure the Backing**

*Stitch a safety pin onto the back of the rosette. Make
sure that you stitch the non-opening side of the pin.*

▲

*Turn a rosette into a
curtain tieback with 2
yards (2m) of 1¹/₂"
(39mm) wide ribbon for the sash. Tie
it in a bow around the curtain. Sew a curtain
ring behind the bow. Slip the ring over a cup
hook attached to the wall. This will prevent the
tie-back from slipping down the curtain. Pin the
rosette onto the bow. Or dress up a plain moiré
pillow with an ambassador-style sash. Wrap a
band of wide ribbon around a pillow, then pin
a rosette onto the sash.*

Flowers made from spiralled pieces of wired ribbon have a generous "cabbage rose" appearance, and they couldn't be simpler to make. Fine lengths of wire are woven into the ribbon edges, giving it resilience and "memory." Pin this rose onto a dress or coat, or use it as a curtain tie-back, an embellishment on a special gift or to top a padded lingerie hanger or keepsake box. You'll really enjoy working with this fun ribbon!

ribbon rose

Ribbon

- ⅝ yard (50cm) of 1½" (39mm) wide hombre (shaded from light to dark) wire-edge taffeta ribbon
- ¾ yard (70cm) of ⅝" (15mm) wide green wire-edge taffeta ribbon

Supplies

- needle and thread
- safety pin
- craft glue
- wooden toothpick

1 | Seal the Ends

Cut a piece of ribbon about 20" (50cm) long. Tease the end of the wire on what will be the inner edge of the rose. Seal the edges by applying craft glue with a toothpick.

2 | Pull the Wire

Grasp the wire and gently push the ribbon down its length, forming gathers.

3 | Coil the Exposed Wire

Wind the wire end around a wooden toothpick to form a small coil, then remove the toothpick. This will prevent you from pulling through the whole length of wire.

4 | Form the Rosebud

Wind the ribbon end around the toothpick several times to form the bud. Remove the toothpick. With doubled sewing thread, catch the base of the coil with a few stitches.

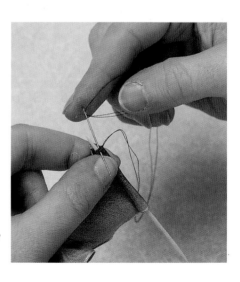

5 Spiral the Ribbon

Begin to form the rose by winding the gathered ribbon in a loose spiral. Reinforce this shape with overcast stitches on the bottom edge as you go.

6 Finish the Bloom

When you reach the end of the ribbon, fold it diagonally, as shown. Stitch the short end onto the base of the rose.

7 Begin the Double-Leaf Pair

Cut two 12" (30cm) pieces of ⁵⁄₈" (15mm) wide wire-edge ribbon. Seal the ends with glue. Fold one piece of the ribbon in half so the ends meet at the center. Open out and flatten the ribbon, forming points at each end. Using matching sewing thread, stitch each point to secure it into position. Repeat for the other piece.

8 Bind the Leaves in the Center

Cut a 3" (8cm) piece of green ribbon and seal the ends. Wrap it around the double-leaf pair at the center, catching the ends of the ribbon. Stitch the center wrap to itself on the wrong side of the leaves.

9 Sew Leaves to the Rose

Center the leaves on the back of the rose and stitch them into place. Stitch along each side of the center wrap. With doubled thread, stitch the non-opening side of a safety pin onto the back of the rose.

If you use hombre ribbon, which is shaded from light to dark along its length, then you can choose to make either a predominantly light-colored or a predominantly dark-colored rose from the same piece of ribbon. Gather the light side for a dark rose, or the dark side for a light rose. They'll complement each other perfectly.

home accents

A splash of color, a hint of texture, a glint of shimmering satin...

These thoughtful details help make a house a home and are part of fond, cherished memories. A touch of ribbon can perk up and personalize your home décor for the kitchen, bed or bath. Add charm to store-bought purchases, and create a friendly, welcoming atmosphere.

Ribbons are both pretty and practical, giving high style and low maintenance. Satin floral trims on a towel or pillowcase, grosgrain appliqués on table linen, or a velvety bow on a pillow or curtain tieback are luxurious extras that family and friends will appreciate at your home. The best part is, all of these fabric projects can be machine washed and no-iron if you label-check the ribbon bolt for easy-care features when you shop.

This section includes a mix of projects using a variety of easy and enjoyable ribboncraft techniques. Try your hand at simplified ribbon weaving with our Amish heart placemats, lace a leaf-motif lampshade, or decorate a dish towel with colorful ribbon flowers.

Projects

Nosegay Towel

✣

Give plain towels a new look by adding a ribbon

border and floral corsage. Sewing on ribbon borders is

simple. Making the pin-on bouquet is also quick and

easy when using purchased ribbon rosebuds. When it's

laundry time, remove the nosegay from the towel. To wash

the nosegay, put it in a mesh laundry bag. Nosegay towels

make delightful housewarming gifts. Make some for

yourself, too—no need to save them only for guests.

Ribbon

- 1¼ yards (1.2m) of 1" (25mm) wide lilac single-face satin ribbon
- ¼ yard (20cm) of ⅛" (3mm) wide violet double-face satin ribbon
- ½ yard (50cm) of ¼" (7mm) wide violet double-face satin ribbon
- ¼ yard (20cm) of 1½" (4cm) wide scalloped white lace
- satin rosebuds, 3 lilac, 3 violet and 1 white

Supplies

- 1 white terrycloth washcloth
- iron-on interfacing
- fabric glue or liquid seam sealant
- small safety pin
- needle and thread
- iron
- straight pins

SEWING MACHINE REQUIRED

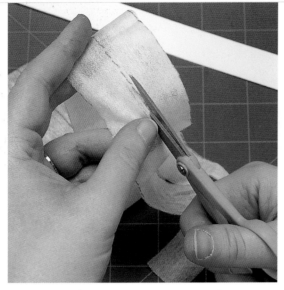

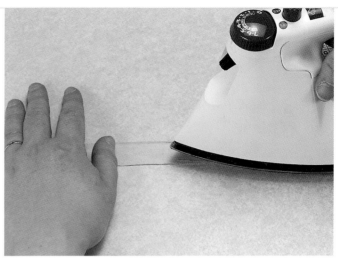

1 Cut Interfacing Strips

To prevent the ribbon from puckering when it is sewn, iron-on interfacing must be applied. Start by cutting strips of interfacing that are ⅛" (3mm) narrower than the actual ribbon width. To do this, cut out a cardboard template to the required width. Trace the strips onto the interfacing, then cut them out.

2 Iron Interfacing Onto the Ribbon

Following the manufacturer's instructions, iron the interfacing strips onto the wrong side of the ribbon.

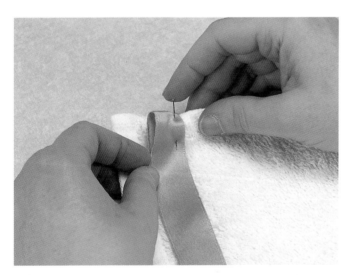

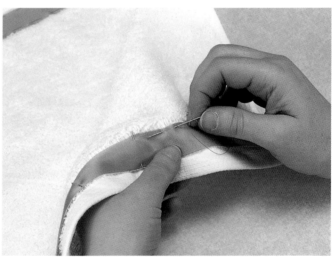

3 Pin the Ribbon Onto the Washcloth

Cut two 9" (23cm) pieces of 1" (25mm) wide lilac ribbon. Pin the ribbon onto the washcloth, covering the woven bands at either side. Tuck the ribbon under ¾" (2cm) at both ends.

4 Baste the Ribbon

Baste stitch the ribbon close to the edges of the washcloth, then remove the pins.

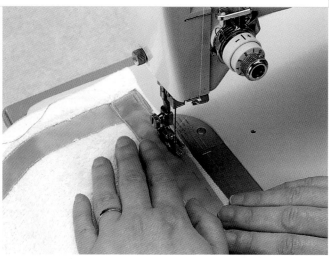

5 | **Stitch the First Ribbon Border**

Use a sewing machine to sew each ribbon close to the edge. Knot the thread on the wrong side and trim close to the knots.

6 | **Continue to Sew Ribbon Borders**

Pin, baste, then sew the two remaining ribbon borders onto the washcloth.

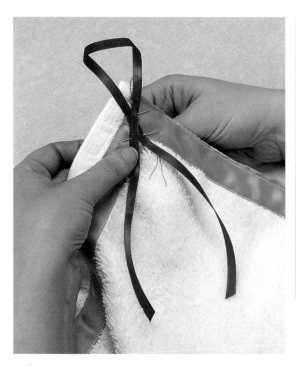

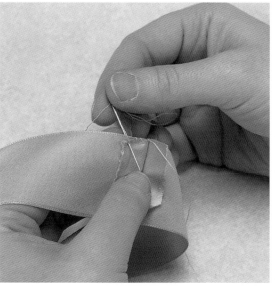

8 | **Make a Loop for the Rosette**

Cut an 8" (20cm) piece of 1" (25mm) wide ribbon. Machine-stitch the short ends of the ribbon together to secure the loop, using a 1/2" (12mm) seam. Finger-press the seam open. Stitch across the seam so it lies flat. Trim the seam bottoms diagonally and seal the cut edges.

7 | **Pin a Hanging Loop in the Corner**

With 18" (46cm) of 1/4" (7mm) wide violet ribbon, pin a loop and stitch the loop to the towel where the ribbon intersects. Trim and seal the ends.

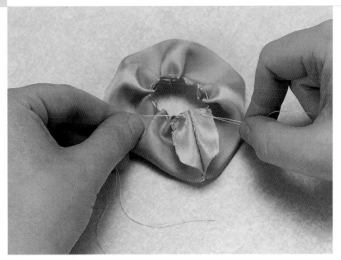

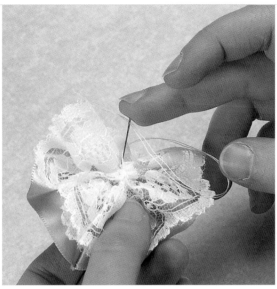

⑨ Gather the Loop

With doubled thread, stitch around the top of the loop. Gently pull up the gathers to form the rosette. Knot, then trim, the thread ends.

⑩ Make a Lace Rosette

Follow steps 8 and 9 to make a rosette out of lace. Place it on top of the ribbon rosette, with centers and seams matching. Sew the rosettes together through the centers.

IT'S A GIFT

Want to make a great gift? Add a ribbon nosegay and trim to a gift basket. Simply glue a wide band of ribbon onto a purchased straw basket. Pin a nosegay onto the band. Line the basket with handmade paper, tissue paper or a paper doily. Fill with scented gift soaps or other small gifts. For presentation, wrap the gift basket in cellophane and tie it with a bow.

⑪ Sew on the Ribbon Rosebuds

Use matching sewing thread to sew on the rosebuds. Place a white rosebud in the center, then alternate lilac and violet around the center rosebud. Sew through the rosebud spirals.

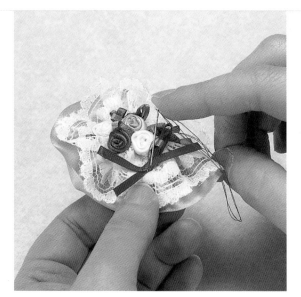

12 | Sew on a Bow

Make a bow using 9" (23cm) of ⅛" (3mm) wide violet ribbon. Seal the ribbon ends. Sew the bow onto the nosegay, stitching through the bow's knot.

13 | Sew a Safety Pin Onto the Back

Stitch the non-opening bar of the safety pin onto the back of the rosette.

Try creating a coordinated set of towels. They're even easier to make—you only have two borders to sew. Choose ribbon wide enough to conceal the towel band. Enlarge the rosette to match the towel's size. You'll need 11" (28cm) of 1½" (4cm) wide satin ribbon for the rosette, and the same quantity of white scalloped lace.

Laced-Leaf Lampshade

This store-bought lampshade makeover yields great

results quickly and inexpensively. It's amazing what a

few paper cut-outs and a bit of simple stitching can do.

When the lamp is switched on, the translucent portion of

the leaves glows softly. This project features a shade for a

table lamp, but you could just as easily decorate a wall

sconce or an ordinary hanging shade. While you're at it,

why not make a matching window shade border?

Ribbon

Ribbon quantities depend on shade dimensions. Here's how to calculate your needs:

- For the top lacing, you need 3 times the top circumference of the shade.

- For the bottom lacing, you need $2^1/2$ times the bottom circumference of the shade.

- For each leaf, use $3/4$ yard (70cm) of $1/8$" (3mm) wide satin ribbon.

For the 10" x 10" (25cm x 25cm) shade shown in this project, use these ribbon quantities:

- $4^1/8$ yards (3.8m) of $1/8$" (3mm) wide moss green double-face satin ribbon for the top and bottom lacing

- 9 yards (8.4m) of $1/8$" (3mm) wide forest green double-face satin ribbon for the leaves

Supplies

- 1 large sheet of green watercolor paper
- 1 large sheet of green vellum
- 10" x 10" (25cm x 25cm) square paper or fabric-covered plastic lampshade
- two frosted seafoam green glass beads
- paper edger scissors, wave pattern
- tapestry needle
- needle and thread
- craft glue
- glue stick
- tape measure
- pencil

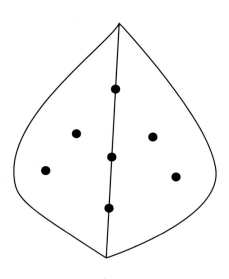

Use this template to make the leaves for the Laced-Leaf Lampshade. It appears here at full size.

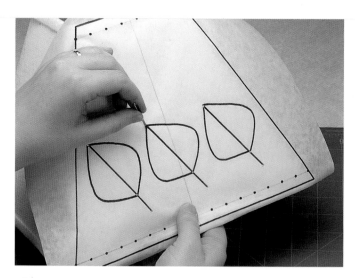

1 Make a Paper Pattern

Because your lampshade may be different from mine, plan the design on paper. Trace around the outline of the shade onto a piece of paper. Using the leaf template to the left, plan the placement of the leaves and the top and bottom lacing holes on the tracing. To mark the leaf positions on the shade, place the pattern over the shade and pierce the shade at the top and bottom of each leaf with a tapestry needle. Also, pierce a hole for the stem bottom, about ³/₄" (2cm) below the leaf bottom.

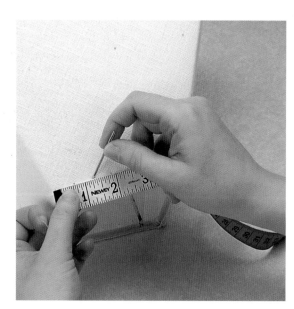

2 Pierce the Lacing Holes

Measure across the shade top and bottom edges. With a tapestry needle, pierce holes at regular intervals, approximately ⁵/₈" (1.5cm) apart.

3 Prepare the Leaves

For each leaf, you need a two-toned piece of paper slightly larger all around than the leaf template. To make the two-toned paper, use a glue stick to glue a right triangle measuring 3¹/₂" (9cm) tall and 2¹/₂" (6cm) long of watercolor paper onto a 3¹/₂" x 2¹/₂" (9cm x 6cm) rectangle of green translucent paper. Using the leaf template above, cut a leaf out of cardstock and pierce the dots with a tapestry needle. Center the cardstock leaf on the two-toned paper and pencil around it, also marking the dots. Pierce dots in the two-toned paper using a tapestry needle. Use paper edgers to cut out the top half of the leaves, and plain scissors to cut out the bottom edges. Cut out as many leaves as required for the shade. This shade requires twelve leaves.

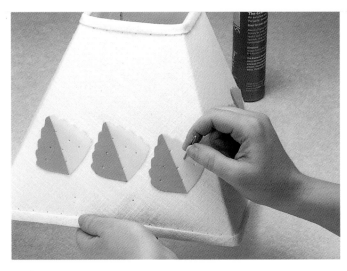

4 Glue the Leaves Onto the Shade

Only glue the bottom half of each leaf (the opaque portion) onto the shade. Position each leaf on the shade, using the shade holes you pierced in step 1 as guides. After each leaf is glued, use a tapestry needle to pierce the lacing holes inside each leaf. Insert a needle through the pierced holes in each paper leaf, penetrating the lampshade material underneath.

5 Start Lacing

Fold a 27" (70cm) piece of ⅛" (3mm) forest green ribbon in half and tie a knot at the center. Thread a tapestry needle with the ribbon doubled. Sew the knot through the top leaf hole.

6 Lace the Leaf

Re-thread the needle with one strand of the ribbon. Make the long stitch at the top of the leaf, then backstitch the vein to the right. Continue stitching the righthand side of the leaf.

7 Stitch the Stem

Make the long stitch that extends from the leaf onto the shade. Then bring the needle back up through the hole at the leaf base. Remove the ribbon from the needle as shown.

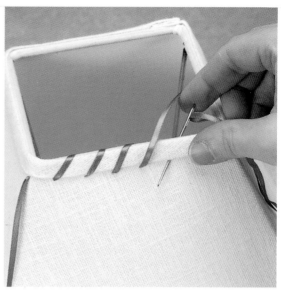

8 | Finish Stitching the Leaf

Re-thread the needle with the remaining ribbon length, then backstitch the lefthand side of the leaf. Bring the ribbon out at the bottom leaf hole, then tie the ribbon ends in a bow. Stitch through the knot with matching sewing thread. Lace all the leaves in this way.

9 | Lace the Top Border

Starting at a corner, lace the top of the shade. Thread the ribbon through the corner hole, leaving a 16" (40cm) tail extending outside the shade. Stitch the ribbon through the holes, angling the stitches.

10 | Complete the Lacing

Work around the top of the shade, bringing the last stitch out through the first hole. Leave a ribbon tail.

11 | Tie a Bow

Pull the ribbon tails tightly and tie them into a bow. To secure the bow, make a stitch through the knot with matching thread.

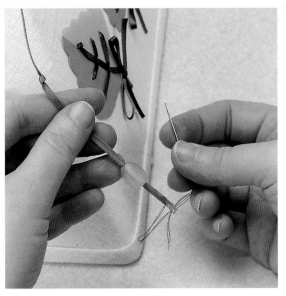

12 Add the Frosted Beads

Knot each ribbon tail to mark the level of each bead. Sew a loop of sewing thread on the ribbon tail and pull it tightly. Re-thread the needle and add one bead. Slide the bead onto the ribbon. The ribbon should pass easily through the bead hole. Knot the ribbon below the bead. Trim the excess ribbon. Repeat for the other bead.

13 Lace the Bottom of the Shade

Stitch the bottom edge of the shade, just as you did for the top of the shade, but omitting the ribbon tails. To finish, knot the ribbon ends inside the shade, and then trim the ribbon.

variation idea

How about an autumn leaves shade to complement the springtime version? Simply change the color scheme for an entirely new project. Try using a round shade for variation as well. To make a pattern tracing of a cylindrical shade, roll the shade along a piece of tracing paper, penciling along the top and bottom edges. A curved pattern will result. Use the pattern to plan the leaf and lacing placement.

This lampshade gives off a soothing glow and is perfect to complement your springtime décor.

Granny Patchwork Pillow

If you want to put a new spin on a traditional idea,

then this is the project for you. Fun and easy to make, this

pillow is a great way to use up small quantities of ribbon

and felt. This is a unit-pieced project. That is, the individual

hexagons build up to form the big center medallion. The

pillow is made of machine-washable felt, which comes in a

vast and sophisticated range of colors. You could also

make a luxury version of the pillow in faux suede.

Ribbon

- 15" (38cm) pieces of ⁵/₈" (15mm) wide satin ribbon, one of each color: dusty rose, burgundy, cream, lilac, purple and moss green
- 47" (1.2m) pieces of ¹/₈" (3mm) wide satin ribbon for the blanket stitching, one of each color: dusty rose, burgundy, cream, lilac, purple and moss green
- 8" (20cm) pieces of ¹/₈" (3mm) wide satin ribbon, one of each color: dusty rose, burgundy, cream, lilac, purple and moss green
- 4¹/₄ yards (4m) of ¹/₈" (3mm) wide satin ribbon in moss green

Supplies

- one 9" x 12" (23cm x 31cm) rectangle each of assorted felt in Leaf Green, Deep Rose, Lavender and Wheat (I chose Kunin Rainbow Classic Felt)
- 1 yard (1m) of Ruby felt
- 1 yard (1m) of 12oz. (340g) polyester batting
- fusible web
- ¹/₁₆" (1.6mm) circle hand punch
- craft knife and cutting mat
- tapestry needle
- masking tape
- needle and thread
- straight pins
- iron

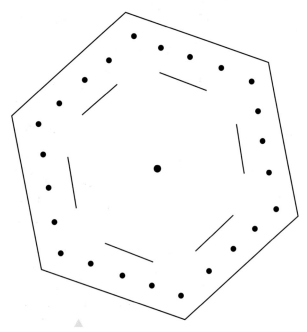

Use this template to make the Granny Patchwork Pillow. Enlarge 111% for the patches. Enlarge 200%, then 200%, then 120% for the pillow cover.

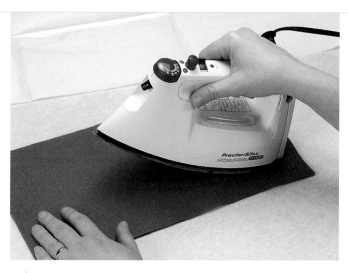

1 Fuse a Double Layer of Felt

The hexagons require double-thick felt. Cut all the felt rectangles in half, crosswise. Following the manufacturer's instructions, sandwich fusible web between two pieces of like-colored felt and bond with a hot iron. Do this with all the hexagon colors.

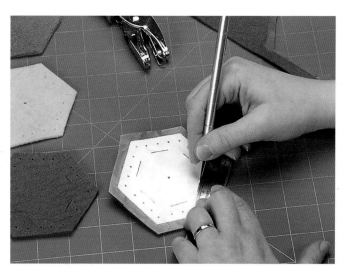

2 Cut Out the Felt Hexagons

Use the hexagon pattern above, and cut hexagons from the double-thick felt: two rose, two lavender, two green and one wheat. To do this, tape the template onto the felt and cut it out. With a craft knife, cut six slits where marked on the template. Next, punch the holes along the edges of the hexagon with a circle hand punch. Use a tapestry needle or nail to pierce the center hole (the hand punch won't reach). Make sure that the center hole is generously sized. You can use small scissors to enlarge it slightly.

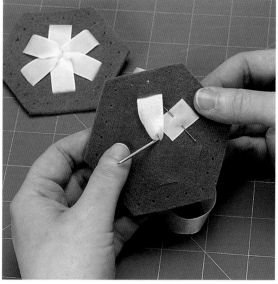

3 Make the Pinwheel Design

Slide a 15" (38cm) piece of ⅝" (15mm) satin ribbon through any slit and pin the end down. Thread the tapestry needle with the free end of the ribbon. Working in a counter-clockwise direction on the wrong side of the hexagon, thread the ribbon up through center hole, then down through the corresponding slot, progressing in a spiral motion. Make sure the ribbon lies flat. When the pinwheel is complete, overlap the ribbon ends and sew them down. Remove the pin.

4 Embroider a French Knot

Bring an 8" (20cm) length of ribbon up through the center hole, then remove the needle. Make five spiral wraps around the needle with the ribbon.

tip *You may want to use a button or bead instead of a French knot to add texture to the pillow.*

5 Complete the French Knot

Insert the needle tip in the center hole. Thread the needle, then gently push the needle through to the other side. Knot and trim the ribbon ends on the wrong side of the hexagon. To prevent the knot from slipping through the center hole, take a few stitches through the knot in matching sewing thread. Catch in all the layers—knot, ribbon and felt.

6 Create a Blanket Stitch Border

Thread the needle with 47" (1.2m) of ⅛" (3mm) wide satin ribbon in a contrasting color. Bring the needle up through a corner hole. Take the needle down through the next hole, then up through the left side of the loop. Continue stitching in this way around the hexagon.

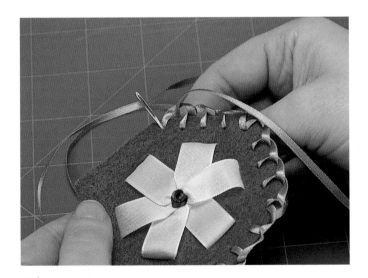

7 Double Stitch the Corners

Stitch twice through the corner holes. This creates a V-formation.

BALANCING THE COLORS

Here's how to arrange ribbon colors successfully within the pillow: Match light hexagons with dark blanket stitching and dark hexagons with light blanket stitching. Ribbon color should contrast sufficiently with the felt hexagon color. Do not place two identical (or very similar) colors next to each other. You may wish to plan the color arrangement on paper before you begin stitching the patchwork together.

8 | Connect the Hexagons

Seven hexagons make up the front of the pillow—six surround the center hexagon. Note the color sequence: lilac, green, pink, repeat (wheat in center). To start, you only need to sew the corners at the base of each surrounding hexagon onto the center hexagon. Make tacking stitches (see page 18) using matching doubled sewing thread. Knot and trim the thread on the wrong side.

9 | Finish the Patchwork

After the hexagons have been sewn onto the center, join them side to side at their top corners.

10 | Blanket Stitch the Pillow Cover

Enlarge the hexagon pattern on page 44. Cut out two hexagons in Ruby felt. Punch 18 border holes per side, spaced 1/2" (12mm) apart and 1/4" (6mm) from the edge. Sew the medallion, centered, onto one piece of felt. Baste the two felt hexagons together on top of each other with edges matching. Blanket stitch through both layers of felt, leaving just over one side of the hexagon unstitched.

11 | Make Your Own Pillow Form

Use the pillow cover pattern to cut three layers of batting. Stack the batting hexagons on top of each other and baste the edges. Stitch the edges of the batting to complete the pillow form. Remove the basting. This is an easy method to make pillow forms in any shape you need.

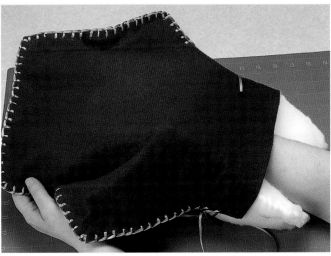

12 | Stuff the Pillow

Insert the pillow form into the felt cover, matching the corners. Blanket stitch the remaining side of the cover. To finish blanket stitching, knot the ribbon on the wrong side of the pillow, then poke the knot through to the inside.

variation idea

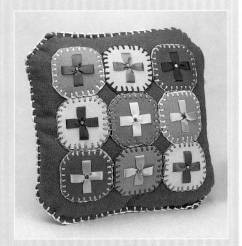

Instead of making a hexagon pillow, create a square pillow with square patchwork. The basic technique is the same as for the hexagon, only you use a total of nine patches. The corners of the square have been trimmed away, which allows the backing fabric to peek through attractively when a group of squares are joined.

This decorative patchwork pillow will make a beautiful addition to any room.

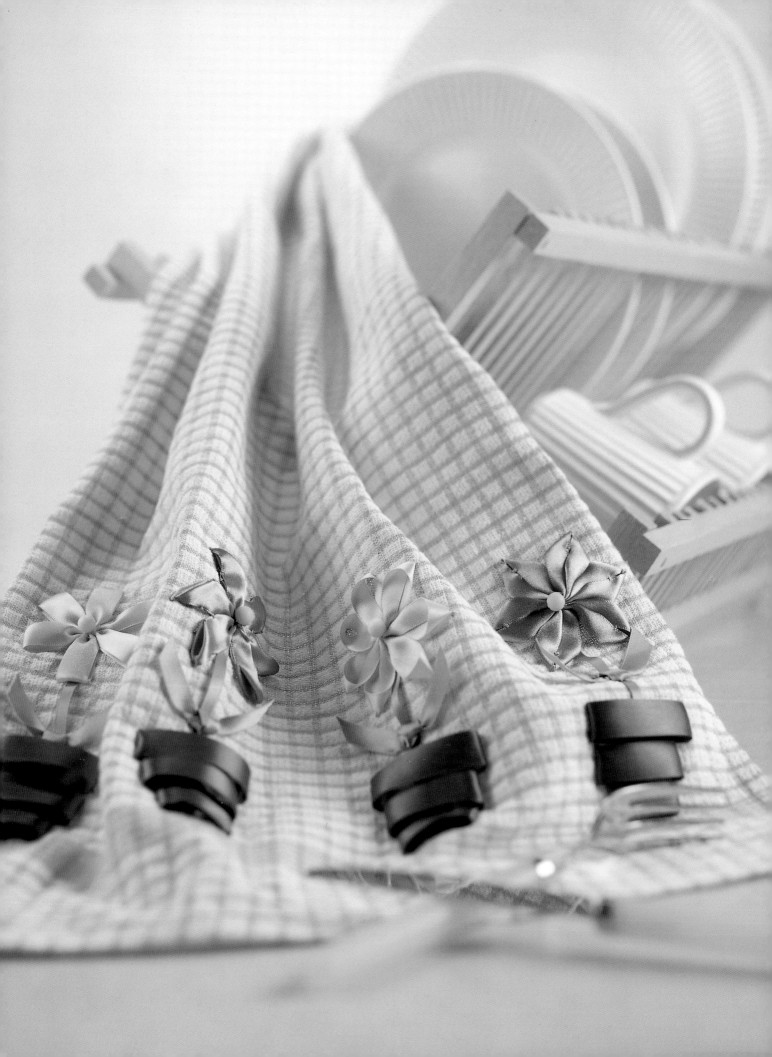

Flowerpot Kitchen Towel

Transform a plain kitchen towel into a decorative

accent using easy, low-sew ribbon appliqués. This towel

features five ribbon flower styles, all made in the same

way, with slight design variations. Simply string the

ribbon petals, then pull up the gathers to complete each

flower. Make it easy. Choose a plaid or checked kitchen

towel for your project—the grid simplifies appliqué

placement, making ribbons easy to space and align.

Ribbon

- $1/2$ yard (50cm) of $5/8$" (15mm) wide blue double-face satin ribbon
- $1 1/8$ yards (1m) of $3/8$" (9mm) wide blue double-face satin ribbon
- $5/8$ yard (50cm) of $1/4$" (7mm) wide leaf green double-face satin ribbon
- $3/4$ yard (60cm) of $3/8$" (9mm) wide leaf green double-face satin ribbon
- $1 3/4$ yards (1.5m) of $5/8$" (15mm) wide terra cotta double-face satin ribbon
- $1/2$ yard (40cm) of $5/8$" (15mm) wide yellow double face satin ribbon
- $5/8$ yard (50cm) of $3/8$" (9mm) wide yellow double-face satin ribbon

Supplies

- 20" x 30" (50cm x 75cm) plaid or checked kitchen towel
- three yellow and two white $1/4$" (7mm) diameter round plastic beads
- needle and thread
- fabric glue or liquid seam sealant
- tape measure
- straight pins

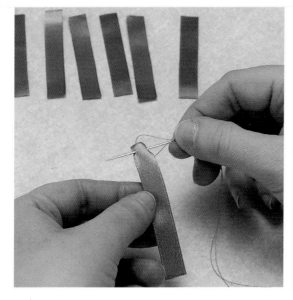

1 Begin the Open-Loop Flower

Cut eight 2³/₄" (6.5cm) strips of ³/₈" (9mm) wide satin blue ribbon. Seal the ends of each strip to prevent fraying (see Finishing Ribbon Edges, page 17). With doubled thread, make a stitch through one end of the ribbon strip.

2 Make a U-Shaped Loop

Sew through the opposite end of the ribbon strip in the same way, forming a U-shaped loop.

3 String the Ribbon Loops into a Ring

To make the flower petals, string all eight ribbon loops together like beads. The rounded side of the loops is the right side. When all eight loops are threaded, turn them to the other side. Sew the last loop to the first loop to complete the circle. Stitch through the base of the first loop.

4 Complete the Flower

Pull the thread tight and knot it securely on the wrong side of the flower. Trim the thread close to the knot.

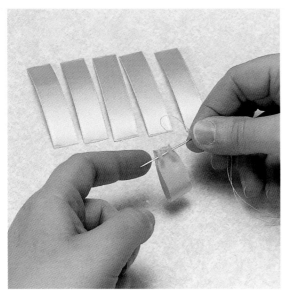

5 Create the Flat-Petal Flower

Cut six 2¹/₂" (6cm) strips of ⁵/₈" (15mm) wide satin yellow ribbon. Seal the strip ends. Fold a strip in half horizontally, to make a loop. With doubled thread, sew three small stitches across the base of the loop: under, over, under.

6 Join the Loops to Form a Ring

Sew all six loops in the same way, and string them like beads as shown. Turn the petals over, then stitch through the first loop to form a ring.

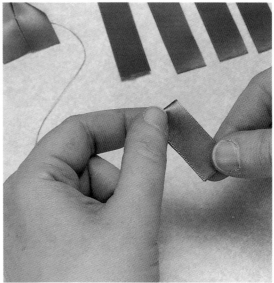

7 Gather and Knot the Petals

Pull the thread tightly, knot it securely and trim the thread close to the knot. The right side of the flower has outwardly-curved petals.

8 Begin the Pinwheel Flower

Of all the flowers, the pinwheel has the most complicated petal shape, but it is easy to make if you take it one step at a time. Cut six 2⁷/₈" (7cm) strips of ⁵/₈" (15mm) wide satin blue ribbon. Crease a strip in half horizontally.

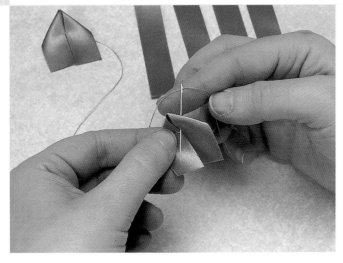

9 Fold into an Inverted V

Open the folded strip, creasing angles at the top to form an inverted V point. Take a few small stitches at the midpoint of the V, catching all of the layers—the right and left sides of the ribbon, plus the layer underneath. The V will now hold its shape permanently.

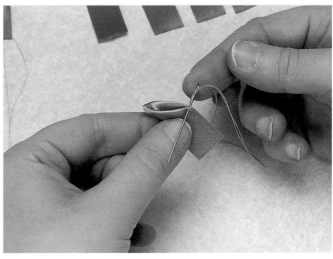

10 Stitch the V Closed

Finger-press the V in half, and stitch the outer corners together to make the angled petal shape. Make five more petals in this way.

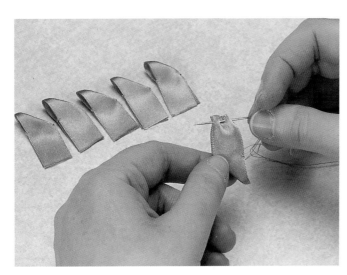

11 Sew Across the Petal Base

Using a doubled piece of thread, make three small stitches across the base of the ribbon loop, as in step 5. String all six petals onto the thread like beads, making sure that the points all face the same direction.

12 Complete the Flower

Sew through the first petal to make a ring. Pull the thread tight to gather the flower, then knot it securely to finish.

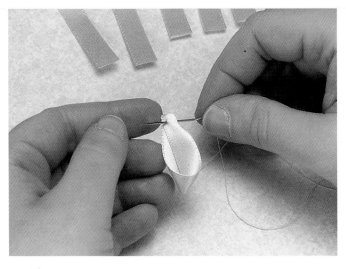

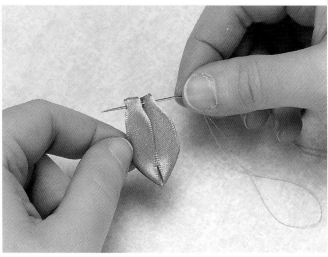

13 Create the Cross-Loop Flower

Cut seven 2³/₄" (7cm) long strips of ³/₈" (9mm) wide satin yellow ribbon. Fold the ribbon into an inverted V, but do not stitch down the point. Slide the righthand ribbon end over the lefthand ribbon end, so that the ends overlap completely. With doubled thread, make a stitch across the overlapped ribbons, as shown. String seven petals together and finish the flower.

14 Create the Starburst Flower

Cut six 2⁷/₈" (7cm) strips of ³/₈" (9mm) wide satin blue ribbon. Fold and stitch an inverted V petal, as in steps 8 and 9. String all six petals and complete the flower.

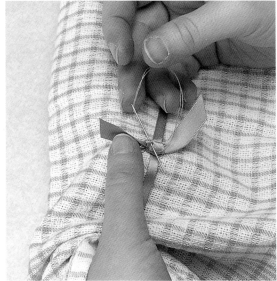

15 Sew Stems on the Towel

Measure across the base of the towel and mark the position of five equally-spaced flower stems with pins. (These stems were spaced 2" [5cm] in from each end and 4" [10cm] apart.) For each stem, cut 3³/₄" (9.5cm) of ¹/₄" (7mm) leaf green satin ribbon, and seal the ends. Pin each stem onto the towel, starting ³/₄" (2cm) above where the flowerpot base will be. Sew each stem onto the towel with tacking stitches at the top and bottom.

16 Add the Leaves

For each pair of leaves, cut 5" (12cm) of ³/₈" (9mm) wide satin leaf green ribbon. Make a center knot. Trim the leaves at an angle, about 1" (2.5cm) to either side of the knot. Seal the ribbon ends. Pin the leaves over the midpoint of the stem. Sew the leaves on the towel, stitching both sides of the knot.

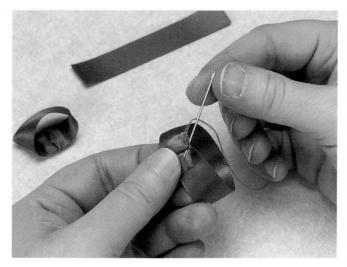

17 Make Flowerpot Loops

Each flowerpot consists of three ribbon loops in graduated sizes. Each flowerpot requires three strips of ⅝" (15mm) wide satin terra cotta ribbon in 4⅞" (12cm), 4" (10cm) and 3¼" (8cm) lengths. Seal ribbon ends, then stitch the short ends of each ribbon strip, taking a ¼" (7mm) seam allowance. Finger-press each seam open, then stitch the top and bottom edges of the seam allowances down.

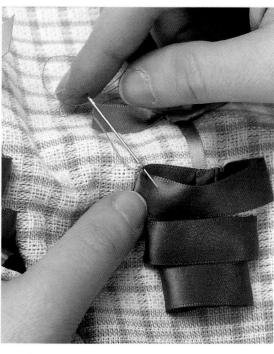

18 Sew on the Flowerpots

Finger-press each loop flat, with the seam at the center back, and pin the stacked flowerpot formation onto the towel, covering the base of each stem. Center all of the loops, going from smallest to largest, as shown. To sew each loop onto the towel, stitch the top and bottom corners.

19 Sew on the Flowers

Pin each flower onto the towel, concealing the top of each stem. Stitch each flower onto the towel through the center. Attach a bead to the center at the same time.

20 Sew Petals Onto the Towel

Catch the ends of each petal with a few stitches to anchor each flower in place.

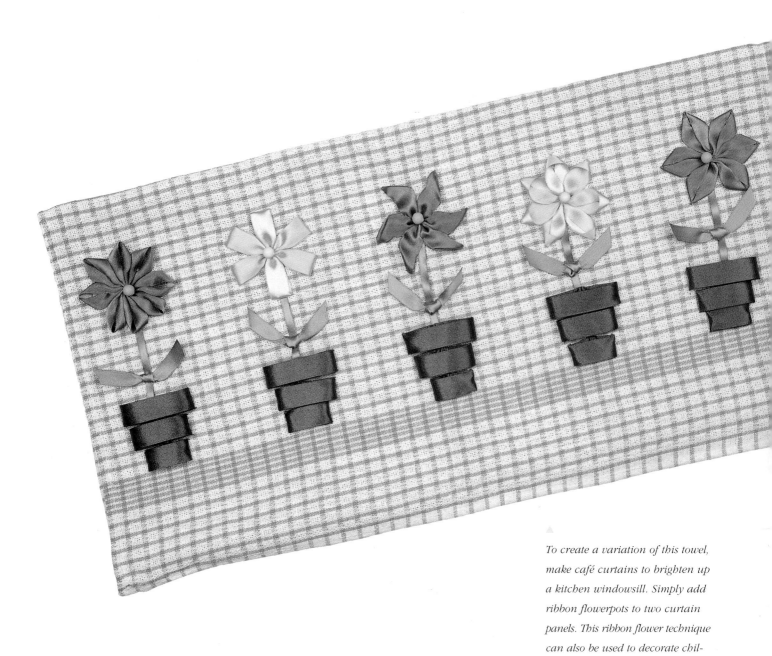

To create a variation of this towel, make café curtains to brighten up a kitchen windowsill. Simply add ribbon flowerpots to two curtain panels. This ribbon flower technique can also be used to decorate children's clothing.

Amish Place Setting

This Amish heart design is applied to woven-ribbon

appliqués, which add a touch of folk art charm and a

splash of color to table accessories. Grosgrain ribbon,

with its subtle crosswise ribs, has been chosen to add

surface texture. It contrasts nicely with the chunky

ridges of the rough-weave placemat. The traditional

Amish colors, brights on a dark background, will add

personality and warmth to your tablesetting.

Ribbon

- 1 1/8 yards (1m) each of 1" (25mm) wide polyester grosgrain ribbon in blue and magenta
- 1 1/4 yards (1.2m) each of 5/8" (15mm) wide polyester grosgrain ribbon in blue and magenta
- 5/8 yard (60cm) of 7/8" (23mm) wide lilac double-face satin ribbon
- 1 1/8 yards (1m) of 1/4" (7mm) wide lilac double-face satin ribbon
- 3 3/4 yards (3.2m) of 1/8" (3mm) wide lilac double-face satin ribbon

Supplies

- 18" x 13" (45cm x 33cm) navy blue placemat
- 15" x 15" (38cm x 38cm) navy blue napkin
- straw basket with 8 1/2" (22cm) diameter opening
- needle and thread
- straight pins
- fabric glue or liquid seam sealant
- tape measure

▶ MATERIALS ARE FOR ONE PLACEMAT, ONE NAPKIN RING AND ONE BASKET.

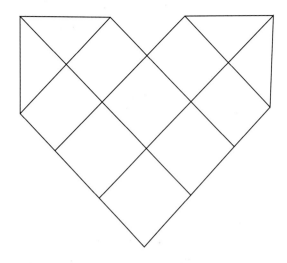

Use this template to make the hearts for the Amish Place Setting. Enlarge 143%.

1 Cut Two Ribbon Strips

Copy the heart template below. Cut one 10" (25cm) piece of magenta 1" (25mm) wide ribbon, and one 10" (25cm) piece of blue ribbon. Fold the blue strip in half crosswise.

2 Fold the Ribbon Points

Open the ribbon loop, creasing angles at the top to form an inverted V. Finger-press it flat, and pin it into place. Stitch through the point, catching both ribbon tails and the base of the triangle. Repeat steps 1 and 2 with the magenta ribbon.

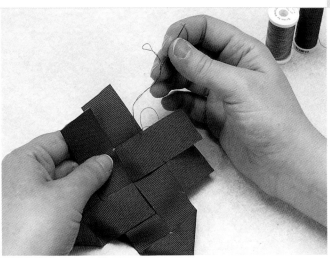

3 | Weave the Ribbon Heart

Weave the two ribbon pairs over, under, under, over, as shown. Hold the woven ribbon against the template to check ribbon positions. Pin the completed weaving.

4 | Stitch the Outer Edges of the Weaving

Secure the cross-points of the ribbon to the outer edges by making a few stitches through all layers in matching thread. For clean, knot-free sewing, begin stitching with a thread loop, as shown (see page 18).

5 | Complete the Stitching

Pull the ribbon tails through the thread loop, as shown, then re-thread your needle and continue sewing. Knot the thread on the back of the heart, and trim the thread ends.

6 | Sew Down the Ribbon Tails

Fold the ribbon tails onto the wrong side of the heart. Pin them in place, then stitch the edges down. Make sure the stitching does not show on the heart front.

7 | Add a Lilac Bow

Tie a bow with 10" (25cm) of ¼" (7mm) ribbon. Trim and seal the ends. Sew it onto the center of the heart. A few stitches at the knot corners will secure it. Make three more woven-ribbon hearts in the same way.

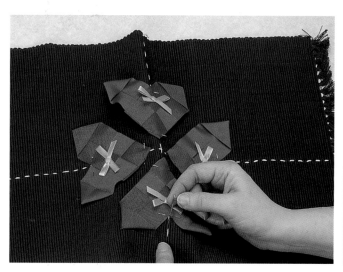

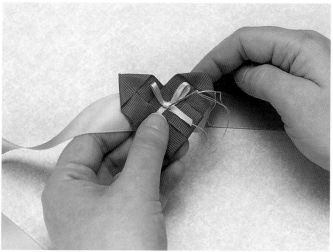

8 | Sew the Hearts Onto the Placemat

Mark the vertical and horizontal center of the placemat with two lines of running stitches. Pin the hearts onto the placemat, points facing center. Make sure they are evenly spaced. Stitch the hearts onto the mat. You only need to stitch the hearts at the points and corners.

9 | Make a Napkin Ring

For a tie-style napkin ring, make a small woven heart and sew it onto the center of a 22" (56cm) strip of ⅞" (23mm) wide lilac ribbon. To make a small woven heart, use 6" (15cm) each of ⅝" (15mm) wide magenta and blue grosgrain. Sew on a bow using 8" (20cm) of ⅛" (3mm) lilac satin.

10 | Attach the Hearts to the Basket

For the basket, make six small woven hearts, as you did for the napkin ring in step 9. Sew a 12" (30cm) piece of ⅛" (3mm) lilac ribbon onto the back of a small woven heart. Knot the ribbon at its midpoint, then stitch through the knot. Thread the ribbon tie through the woven straw of the basket. Repeat for each heart, spacing them apart evenly. Tie bows on the inside of the basket to secure the ties.

You can make an entire coordinated tabletop ensemble using the Amish heart appliqués. Sew them onto napkins, a tablecloth or a table runner. Consider creating festive Christmas ornaments using red and green grosgrain.

Ribbon Embroidered Desk Set

✣

Capture the look of smocking by doing a few simple ribbon

embroidery stitches on corrugated cardboard. This desk set

combines the ease of papercrafting with the elegance of

needlework. The ridges of the corrugated cardboard teamed

with the pre-pierced stitching holes make spacing your

stitching simple. A variety of stitches are used for this project,

so think of it as a ribbon embroidery sampler. This pretty,

pastel desk set would look great in a girl's bedroom.

1 Ink Blotter • *page 64*

Ribbon

- 1 yard (90cm) of ¹/₈" (3mm) wide cream double-face satin ribbon
- 4 yards (3.8m) of ¹/₈" (3mm) wide lavender double-face satin ribbon
- 1¹/₄ yards (1.1m) of ¹/₈" (3mm) wide pink double-face satin ribbon
- 2³/₈ yards (2.1m) of ¹/₈" (3mm) wide turquoise double-face satin ribbon

Supplies

- 13¹/₄" x 6" (33.5cm x 15cm) cream corrugated cardboard
- 18" x 13" (46cm x 33.5cm) cream illustration board
- 1 sheet each of pink and turquoise pearlescent cardboard
- 11⁵/₈" x 15¹/₂" (30cm x 39cm) pink blotter paper
- paper edger scissors, clouds pattern
- 1" (2.5cm) diameter flower-shaped hand punch
- craft knife and cutting mat
- tapestry needle
- needle and thread
- craft glue

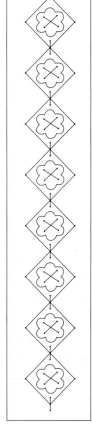

Use this template to make the Ink Blotter. Enlarge 200%.

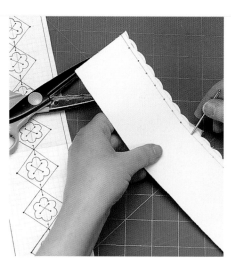

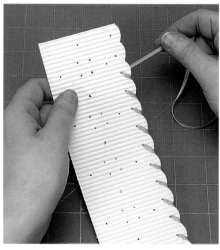

1 Prepare the Blotter Strips

Using the template provided, cut two strips of cream-colored corrugated cardboard to 13¼" (33.5cm) long, cutting one long edge with paper edgers. On the smooth side of the cardboard, pierce holes along the scalloped edge. Also, pierce the remaining stitch holes as shown on the pattern.

2 Stitch the Scalloped Edge

Thread the tapestry needle with 24" (60cm) of turquoise ribbon and stitch the scalloped edge, spiralling ribbon from the center hole over the scallop. Repeat on the second blotter strip. When finished, apply a dab of craft glue to the end of the ribbon and smooth the ribbon onto the back of the blotter strip.

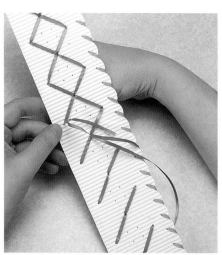

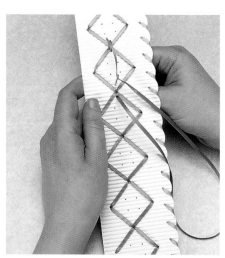

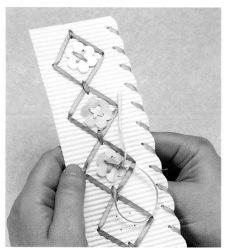

3 Embroider the Lattice Pattern

Thread a tapestry needle with 2 yards (1.9m) of dark lavender ribbon. Work the stitches through the holes in diagonal pairs, going first in one direction, then reversing to complete the diamond lattice. Repeat for the other blotter strip.

4 Stitch the Lattice Intersections

Thread the needle with 22" (56cm) of pink ribbon. Back stitch over each lattice intersection (see page 20). Repeat on the other blotter strip.

5 Sew on the Flowers

Punch out eight turquoise flowers and eight cream flowers from pearlescent paper. Pierce four centered "buttonholes" in each. Make a cross stitch in each flower, using turquoise ribbon for pink flowers and pink ribbon for turquoise flowers. Glue the ribbon ends onto the back.

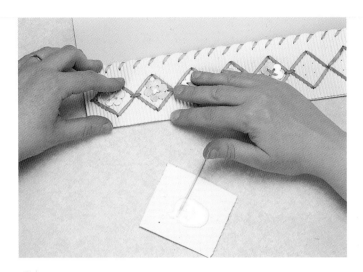

6 Assemble the Blotter

For the blotter backing board, cut a piece of cream-colored illustration board measuring 13" x 18" (33 x 45.5cm). Glue the three straight edges of each blotter strip to the board. Press along the glued edges and weight the blotter with books as it dries. Cut a piece of blotter paper to 11½" x 15½" (29 x 39.5cm) and slip it in place.

The finished Ink Blotter stands on its own as a fashionable project, or works well with other pieces in the desk set.

variation **idea**

Why not make a ribbon-embroidered desk set consisting of several pieces? A plastic cylinder, for example, can easily be transformed into a decorative pencil holder by adding the same design elements as the Ink Blotter. The coordinating pieces will look great in any little girl's room.

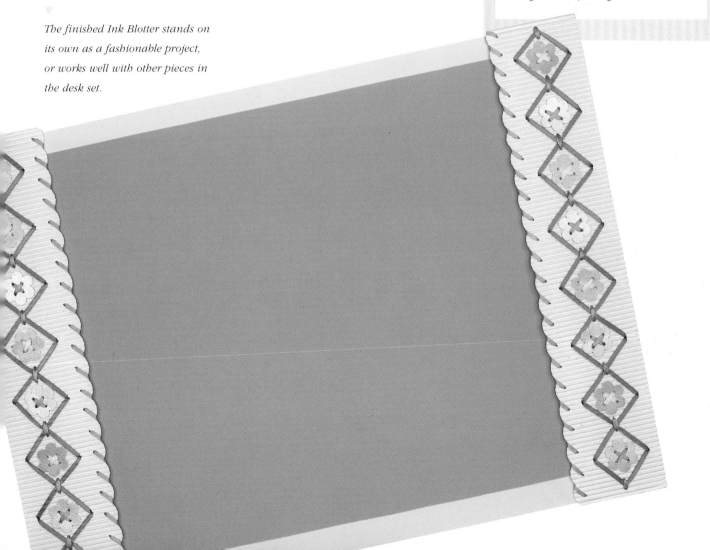

2 Picture Frame

Ribbon

- 1⁵⁄₈ yards (1.5m) of ¹⁄₈" (3mm) wide cream double-face satin ribbon
- 2¹⁄₂ yards (2.2m) of ¹⁄₈" (3mm) wide pink double-face satin ribbon
- 1³⁄₈ yards (1.2m) of ¹⁄₈" (3mm) wide turquoise double-face satin ribbon

Supplies

- 8" x 10" (20cm x 25cm) sheet of lilac corrugated cardboard
- one sheet of cream pearlescent cardboard
- 19" x 23" (48cm x 58cm) sheet of white illustration board or heavyweight cardboard
- paper edger scissors, clouds pattern
- 1" (2.5cm) diameter flower-shaped hand punch
- craft knife and cutting mat
- tapestry needle
- needle and thread
- craft glue

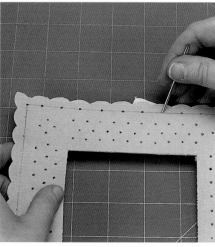

1 Cut Out the Frame and Design

Enlarge template A and copy it onto tracing paper. Tape the pattern onto the smooth side of a piece of corrugated cardboard (on the right side, ridges should run horizontally across the frame). Using a tapestry needle, poke holes at both ends of the marked lines. With a craft knife, cut out the window, and use paper edgers to cut out the frame.

2 Pierce Holes

Using a tapestry needle, pierce holes at the dots and at either end of the marked lines. Also, pierce holes at the scallop mid-point, ³⁄₈" (1cm) below the scallop peak.

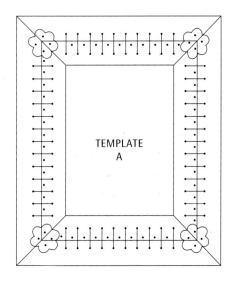

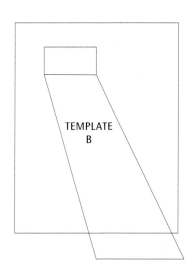

Use template A for the Picture Frame front and surround. Enlarge 200%.

Use template B for the Picture Frame backing piece and strut. Enlarge 200%.

TEMPLATE A

TEMPLATE B

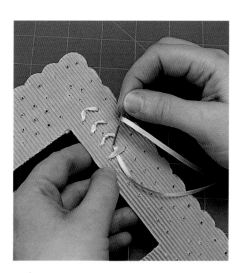

3 Add the Fishbone Embroidery Stitch

Thread a needle with pink ribbon. For each short side of the frame, use 40" (1m), and for each long side, use 48" (1.2m) of ribbon. Starting from a hole near the window cut-out, make a horizontal stitch, left to right. Bring the needle up above the stitch at the center hole. Loop the ribbon under and around the horizontal stitch. Bring the ribbon back down the same center hole. Continue on all four sides of the frame.

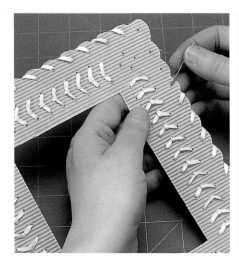 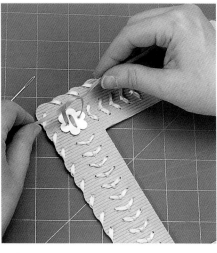 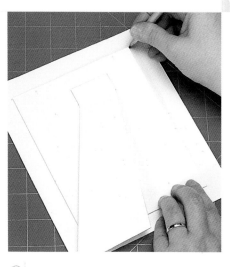

4 Stitch the Frame Edges

Thread the needle with cream ribbon. Stitch around the frame edges, spiralling ribbon from the center hole of each of the scallop valleys. Work in a counterclockwise direction. Glue the ribbon tails down on the wrong side of the frame.

5 Tie on the Corner Bows

Punch four flower shapes from pearlescent cardboard. Pierce four "buttonholes" in each flower, as indicated on the pattern. To sew on each flower, thread a needle with 12" (30cm) of turquoise ribbon. Sew the flower onto the frame, using a diagonal stitch from top right to bottom left of the buttonholes. Sew the ribbon ends through the remaining buttonholes. Tie a bow and secure it with a stitch through the knot with matching sewing thread.

6 Cut Out the Frame Pieces

Enlarge templates A and B and cut out the frame surround, backing piece and strut from cardboard using a craft knife and metal ruler. Score the strut near the top, as marked. Glue the strut top onto the backing piece. Next, apply glue around three edges of the backing piece, leaving the top glue-free so a photo can be inserted. Glue the backing piece onto the frame surround. Glue the corrugated cardboard onto the front of the frame surround, matching the edges. Weight the frame with books as the glue dries.

This photo frame has been designed to fit a snapshot measuring 4" x 6" (10cm x 15cm). Just slip the photo into the slot at the top. The frame can be used in either portrait or landscape direction. Tie the button-bows to face the direction of use.

[section two]

gifts and keepsakes

Say the word gift, and what images spring to your mind?

A ribbon-tied box with a magnificent bow. Ribbons and gift-giving go hand in hand because using ribbon is a simple way to add a festive touch to a special gift or treasured keepsake. When you invest time in crafting a gift, you want it to be special and unique.

This section includes ribboncraft ideas for everyone on your gift-giving list. Some of the projects can be produced quickly and in large quantities as party favors, like the Pomander Sachet. Others, such as the Snowflake Holiday Stocking, are more involved keepsake projects that could be displayed for many years to come.

You'll be inspired by the folk art style of the Amish Papercrafts, and brush up on an Early American tradition with the Beaded Penny Rug Purse. Plus, the Rose Garland Makeup Bag will glamourize your beauty accessories with style and simplicity.

Keepsake Sachets

Transform an ordinary handkerchief into a

dainty sachet. Pretty and practical, these fragrant

sachets loop over a doorhandle to scent your bathroom,

bedroom, or linen closet. There are three different

styles to choose from: the Drawstring Purse Sachet,

the Strawberry Sachet, and the Pomander Sachet.

They all have easily-refillable pouches that hold an

abundance of fragrant potpourri.

1 Drawstring Purse Sachet • *page 72*

Ribbon

- ³/₈ yard (30cm) of ¹/₄" (7mm) wide mint green double-face satin ribbon
- ⁷/₈ yard (80cm) of ¹/₈" (3mm) wide mint green double-face satin ribbon
- 2¹/₈ yards (2m) of ¹/₄" (5mm) wide pink polyester gingham ribbon
- 5 red ribbon rosebuds

Supplies

- 10" x 10" (25cm x 25cm) floral-print handkerchief
- 2 clear red plastic beads
- potpourri
- needle and thread
- straight pins
- small safety pin
- fabric glue or liquid seam sealant
- tape measure

SEWING MACHINE REQUIRED

1 Fold and Stitch the Handkerchief

Fold the hankie so the triangular points meet in the center. Pin it in place. Machine stitch around all four sides of the hankie. Sew two parallel lines of stitching, one close to the folded edge and the other $5/8$" (1.5cm) from the folded edge.

2 Thread the Drawstrings

Cut two pieces of gingham ribbon, each measuring 22" (58cm) long. Pin a small safety pin to one end of a ribbon. Use the pin to guide the ribbon through the stitched channel and across the gap between two sides. When you have threaded the first ribbon, insert the other ribbon through the remaining two sides of the handkerchief.

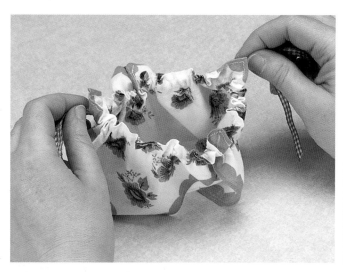

3 Pull Up the Gathers

Pull the drawstring ribbons to gather the handkerchief into a pouch.

4 Add Beads and Knot Ribbons

On each side of the pouch, thread both ribbon ends through a tapestry needle, then thread on a bead. Hold all four ends of the drawstring together and knot them about $2^{1}/2$" (6cm) from the tops of the ribbons. Trim the ribbon ends at an angle and seal them.

5 Add a Bow

Make a bow from 10" (25cm) of ¼" (7mm) mint green ribbon. Pin it in place, and sew it onto the knot. Sew a ribbon rose onto the bow center.

6 Decorate the Handkerchief Points

Cut the ⅛" (3mm) mint green ribbon into four 8" (20cm) lengths. Make a fish loop out of each piece and pin one onto each corner (see page 19 for Fish Loop instructions). Cut four 8" (20cm) pieces of gingham ribbon. Tie bows and sew them over the fish loops. Sew purchased rosebuds near the top corners of the handkerchief points.

Fill the pouch with potpourri and hang it on a bedroom door or place it in a lingerie drawer.

2 Strawberry Sachet

Ribbon

- 1 yard (90cm) of ¼" (5mm) wide pink polyester gingham ribbon
- ³/₈ yard (30cm) each of ¹/₈" (3mm) wide double-face satin ribbon in pink, green and white
- 1 red ribbon rose

Supplies

- ¼ yard (30cm) of tulle
- 10" x 10" (25cm x 25cm) floral-print handkerchief (border print works best)
- 2 clear red plastic beads
- potpourri
- paper edger scissors
- pinking shears
- needle and thread
- straight pins
- small safety pin
- fabric glue or liquid seam sealant
- tape measure

1 Cut and Pin the Pattern

Enlarge the provided templates. Pin the sachet pattern onto a double layer of tulle. Using pinking shears, cut out the tulle. Use the handkerchief point pattern below to cut two opposite corners off the handkerchief. Baste under the seam allowance on the long edge of the hankie and trim off the extending corners. Place the handkerchief corner exactly on top of the pointy end of a tulle piece. Pin it in place.

2 Sew a Drawstring Path

Fold the corners of the tulle and handkerchief to the front and pin down. Machine-stitch a drawstring path across the top. Stitch two parallel lines, one close to the edge, the other with a ⁵/₈" (1.5cm) seam allowance. Stitch only on the handkerchief area—stitching should not extend onto the tulle. Repeat for the other piece of the sachet.

3 Finish the Thread Ends

Thread a needle with the thread ends on the top side of the sachet. Bring the ends to the wrong side. Knot, then trim the thread.

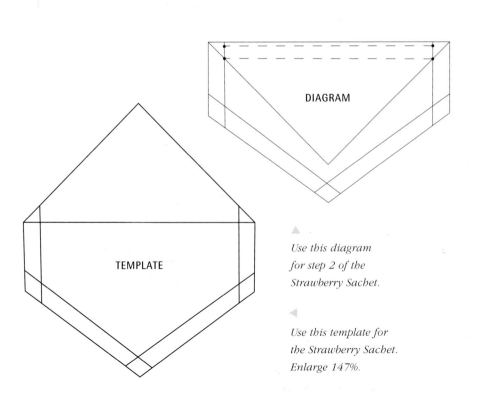

DIAGRAM

TEMPLATE

Use this diagram for step 2 of the Strawberry Sachet.

Use this template for the Strawberry Sachet. Enlarge 147%.

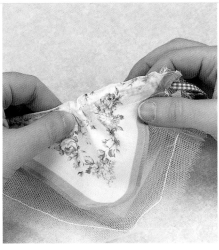

4 Stitch the Sachet

With the wrong sides together and edges even, stitch the sachet front to back. Use a 5/8" (1.5cm) seam allowance. Be sure to begin the stitching below the drawstring path.

5 Thread the Ribbon

Cut the pink gingham ribbon into two 18" (45cm) pieces. Fasten a safety pin to one end of the ribbon, then use it to guide the ribbon through the handkerchief. Repeat on the other side.

6 Thread on the Beads

On each side of the sachet, add a bead, then knot the ribbon ends together. Trim the ends at an angle, then seal them (see page 17).

7 Make a Triple Bow

Cut three 10" (25cm) pieces of 1/8" (3mm) wide ribbon in white, pink and green. Tie a bow, treating all three strands as a single thickness. Fluff the bow.

8 Sew on the Bow

Stitch the bow onto the center top of the sachet. Sew a ribbon rose over the knot.

▷ *Fill the sachet with potpourri. To make a more economical Strawberry Sachet, use only tulle.*

3 Pomander Sachet

Ribbon

- ³/₈ yard (30cm) of ⁵/₈" (15mm) wide cream double-face satin ribbon
- 15" (50cm) of ³/₈" (9mm) wide lilac double-face satin ribbon
- 18" (40cm) of ¹/₄" (7mm) wide lilac double-face satin ribbon
- 1¹/₄ yards (1.1m) of ³/₁₆" (5mm) wide pink feather-edge, double-face satin ribbon
- ³/₈ yard (30cm) of ¹/₈" (3mm) wide pink double-face satin ribbon

Supplies

- ³/₈ yard (30cm) of tulle
- potpourri
- paper edger scissors
- needle and thread
- straight pins
- craft glue

1 Pin Ribbons Onto the Net

Enlarge the template and cover it with tulle. Cut three 7" (18cm) strips of ³/₁₆" (5mm) wide pink feather-edge ribbon. With matching thread, sew the ribbons onto the tulle at the intersecting point and at the end of every piece. Cut out the tulle using paper edgers.

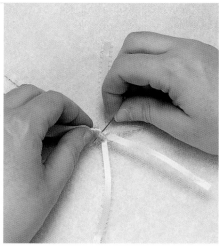

2 Attach the Hanging Loop

Cut a 20" (50cm) piece of ³/₈" (9mm) wide lavender ribbon for the handle. Fold it in half and knot the ends to make a loop. Sew the knot onto the inside center (on the wrong side) of the tulle circle.

3 Sew on the Ribbon Tails

Cut two 15" (38cm) pieces of ¹/₄" (7mm) wide lavender ribbon for the streamers. Put one piece of ribbon on top of the other. Sew the streamers, at their midpoints, onto the outside center of the net circle.

4 Add a Bow

Make a bow from 10" (25cm) of ⁵/₈" (15mm) wide cream satin ribbon. Sew it onto the folded ribbon tails.

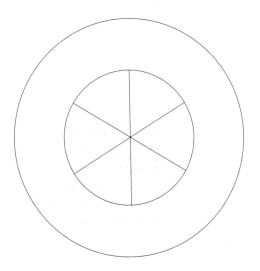

Use this template to make the Pomander Sachet. Enlarge 200%, then 125%.

5 Begin the Drawstring Stitch

Add a running stitch around the "inner circle" of the tulle (stitch just outside the feather-edge ribbon ends). Center the potpourri on the tulle circle. Gently pull up the running stitch thread to gather the tulle, and tie the pouch.

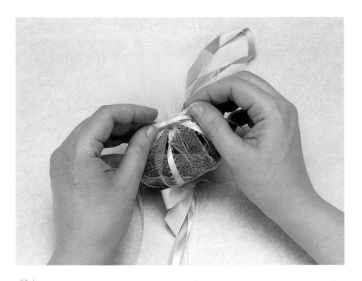

6 Conceal the Gathering With a Bow

Wrap a 12" (30cm) piece of ³/₈" (8mm) wide pink ribbon around the neck of the pouch. Tie the ends into a bow.

Hang this Pomander Sachet from a bedroom door. You may also reduce the template and make a smaller version for a drawer pull.

Snowflake Holiday Stocking

❋

This stocking features an easy-stitch version of net

embroidery, the needlecraft in which delicate stitchery

is worked on openwork mesh fabric. Because the tulle is

backed with felt, the mechanics of your needlework are

kept hidden (where they belong). The border stitch,

a streamlined version of the closed buttonhole stitch,

saves time, too! The embroidery requires a fair amount

of ribbon, but your investment will surely pay off.

Ribbon

- 5/8 yard (50cm) of 5/8" (15mm) wide red double-face satin ribbon
- 1/2 yard (40cm) of 1 1/2" (4cm) wide plaid ribbon
- 20 yards (20m) of 1/8" (3mm) wide white double-face satin ribbon

Supplies

- 3/8 yard (30cm) of machine-washable red felt
- 3/8 yard (30cm) of white tulle or net
- eighteen 1/4" (7mm) diameter frosted white glass beads
- 1/16" (1.6mm) circle hand punch
- chenille needle and tapestry needle
- needle and thread
- straight pins
- black fabric marker
- fabric glue or liquid seam sealant
- tracing paper

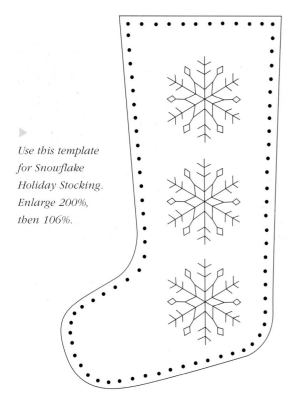

Use this template for Snowflake Holiday Stocking. Enlarge 200%, then 106%.

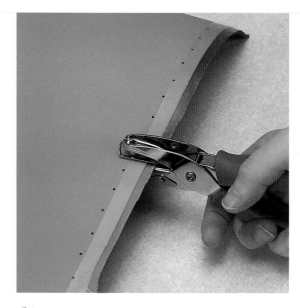

1 Cut the Stocking Out From Felt

Enlarge the stocking pattern to the left. Make a stocking template in heavyweight paper, with dots marked around the edge. Tape the pattern onto red felt, and cut it out roughly. Punch holes at the dots with a 1/16" (1.6mm) circle punch. Cut the stocking shape out of felt. Cut out another felt stocking in the same way (for the stocking back).

2 Mark the Snowflakes on the Tulle

From the stocking pattern, make a tracing paper pattern with the snowflake outlined. Cut a piece of tulle to fit over the tracing. Tape or pin the pattern under the tulle. Outline the snowflakes on the tulle with a black fabric marker. Use a ruler to keep lines straight.

3 Embroider the Snowflake Spokes

Lay the tulle over the felt stocking. Baste around the edges and trim the excess tulle. Thread an embroidery needle with 1/8" (3mm) wide white satin ribbon. Back stitch (see page 20) the snowflake spokes. Make sure your stitching conceals the black outlines, and that the ribbon does not twist. Each snowflake requires about 3 3/4 yards (3.5m) of ribbon.

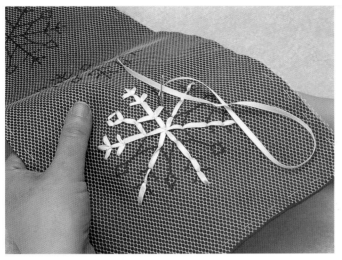

4 | Stitch the Snowflake Details

After the spokes are completed, back stitch the details. Work around each snowflake, one spoke at a time. When stitching is finished, knot and trim the ribbon ends on the wrong side.

tip *When embroidering with ribbon, it is crucial to make sure that the ribbon lies flat. Smooth out any twists before moving on to the next stitch.*

5 | Sew on the Beads

Stitch on a bead just above the tip of each diamond-top spoke (alternate spokes). Using doubled sewing thread, take several stitches through each bead and knot on the wrong side.

6 | Outline the Back

Thread a tapestry needle with ribbon, and with the stocking toe pointing left, stitch the top edge of the back piece. To begin stitching, take a diagonal stitch from the upper lefthand corner down into the righthand hole. Bring the stitch up in the lefthand loop.

Continue by bringing the ribbon down the lower righthand hole again. Pass the ribbon through the loop, then repeat the cycle across the top edge of the stocking, keeping an even tension.

7 | Stitch the Stocking Front to Back

With ribbon, stitch across the top edge of the stocking front, same as for the stocking back (steps 6 and 7), but with stocking toe pointing right. Next join the stocking front to back. Place stocking front on top of the stocking back, with wrong sides together and edges even. Align the holes and stitch all around the stocking, through both layers of felt. Knot the ribbon ends and poke them inside the stocking.

8 | Sew on a Hanging Loop

Cut a piece of ⅝" (15mm) wide red satin ribbon measuring 14" (35cm).
Pin a diagonal fish loop in the lefthand corner of the stocking. Sew the loop
where the ribbon intersects, stitching through all of the layers of ribbon
and stocking. Trim the ribbon ends diagonally and seal with craft glue.

9 | Begin the Bow With a Loop

Cut an 18" (45cm) piece of plaid ribbon. Fold it in half to make a loop. Pin
the ribbon together 6" (15cm) below the fold. Back stitch across the width
of the ribbon through both layers and remove the pin.

10 | Gather the Bow Center

Open the loop and flatten it out with the seam centered.
Thread a needle with doubled sewing thread. Take three small
stitches—under, over, under—then pull the stitches tightly to
gather the ribbon. Knot the thread on the wrong side.

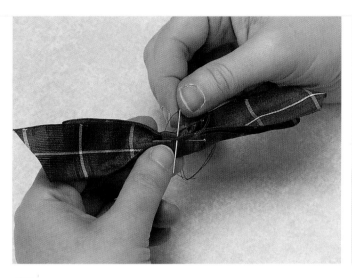

11 Add a Loop Around the Center

Cut a 6" (15cm) piece of red ribbon. Wrap it tightly around the bow center, folding the end under on the wrong side. Stitch the seam. Trim the bow ends diagonally and seal them with craft glue.

12 Sew the Bow Onto the Hanging Loop

Pin the bow onto the hanging loop, concealing the loop's cross points. Sew the bow to the stocking, stitching at the corners of the center loop.

Make a stocking for every family member, and hang them on the mantle for a one-of-a-kind holiday decoration.

Amish Papercrafts

Amish patchwork, prized for its combination of

vibrant, contrasting colors and bold geometric designs,

is the folk art inspiration for this project. The bookmark

provides a simple introduction to ribbon weaving,

along with an opportunity to play with fun papercraft

tools. The notecard features a jumbo version of the

friendship heart motif, and surrounds it with a

hand-stitched, ribbon-laced border.

1 Amish Heart Bookmark • *page 86*

Ribbon

- 5/8 yard (60cm) each of 1/4" (7mm) wide single-face satin ribbon in red and purple
- 5/8 yard (50cm) of 3/8" (9mm) wide double-face satin red ribbon

Supplies

- 1 sheet of black cardstock
- 1 sheet each of red and purple paper
- 1/2" (12mm) heart-shaped paper punch
- 1/8" (3mm) circle hand punch
- craft knife and cutting mat
- needle and thread
- craft glue
- glue stick
- masking tape
- rounded corner edgers (optional)

Use this template for the Amish Heart Bookmark. Enlarge 200%.

1 Trace and Cut Out the Bookmark

Enlarge the template to the left, and trace the pattern. Cut out a piece of black cardstock measuring 8" x 2½" (20cm x 6cm). Tape the tracing over the black card and impress the pattern outlines with a dry fine-point pen. Cut out the three windows with a craft knife and ruler. Round off the top corners with corner edgers. Punch a ⅛" (3mm) hole at the top center of the bookmark.

2 Add the Paper Cut-Outs

Punch out two purple hearts and one red heart from the red and purple paper. Using the bookmark tracing, mark and then cut out three ⅞" (23mm) diameter red semi-circles and three purple ones. Apply a glue stick to the wrong side of each cut-out and smooth the cut-outs in place over the impressed pattern outline.

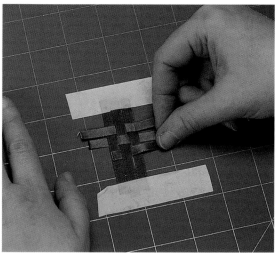

3 Weave the Ribbon

For the woven center, cut six 2½" (6.5cm) strips of ¼" (7mm) wide ribbon, three red strips and three purple. Tape three vertical red strips directly onto the cutting mat. Position the strips face (shiny side) down, side-by-side, with no gaps. Weave the purple ribbons horizontally through the red ribbon. Apply overlapped strips of clear tape to cover and reinforce the weaving, then cut off the masking tape with scissors. Make three woven centers in this way.

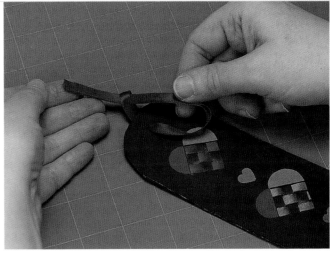

4 Add the Weaving

Position each of the three weavings behind its window, sticky tape side down, and glue it in place. Make sure each weaving fits behind its window squarely. Cut out a backing to exactly match the front of the bookmark and glue it to the wrong side of the bookmark. Punch a top hole in the backing, in the same position as the bookmark front.

5 Loop a Ribbon Tail

Cut a 10" (25cm) piece of ³/₈" (9mm) wide red ribbon for the top tail. Fold the ribbon strip in half, push the loop through the punched hole from front to back. Next, thread the tails through the loop and pull tight to make a "half-hitch" knot. Cut angled edges at the ends of the ribbon. Seal the ribbon edges.

tip   *When making papercrafts with ribbon, buy your ribbon first, then match paper colors to the ribbon. Staple ribbon swatches onto a piece of neutral-colored paper for at-a-glance shopping convenience.*

6 Add a Final Bow

Cut a 10" (25cm) piece of ³/₈" (9mm) wide red satin ribbon. Tie it into a bow, adjust the loops to equal size, then trim and seal the bow ends. Sew a few stitches at the top and bottom of the bow knot to attach the bow to the ribbon tail.

The bright and bold colors on this Amish patchwork heart make a stunning bookmark that you could give as a gift, along with a favorite book, to your family or friends.

2 Amish Heart Notecard

Ribbon

- ½ yard (40cm) each of ⅝" (15mm) wide single-face satin ribbon in red and purple
- 2 yards (1.7m) of ⅛" (3mm) wide red double-face satin ribbon
- ⅛ yard (20cm) of ⅛" (3mm) wide lilac double-face satin ribbon

Supplies

- 2 sheets of lilac parchment-look cardstock
- 1 sheet each of red and purple paper
- 1" (2.5cm) heart-shaped paper punch
- ⅛" (3mm) circle hand punch
- craft knife and cutting mat
- tapestry needle
- needle and thread
- craft glue
- glue stick
- rounded corner edgers (optional)

1 Transfer the Template

Enlarge the notecard pattern for the card front given below and trace the pattern. Tape the tracing over lilac cardstock, and impress the pattern outlines with a dry fine-point pen. Use a ruler for the straight lines. Lightly score the center fold of the card, using a craft knife against the ruler.

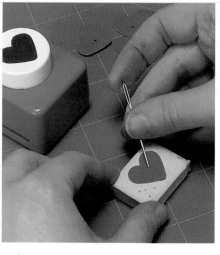

2 Cut Out the Paper Buttons

The heart-shaped buttons must be sturdy, so use a glue stick to mount a small piece of the purple paper onto a piece of the thicker lilac parchment paper. Punch out four hearts. Pierce a center hole in each heart using a tapestry needle.

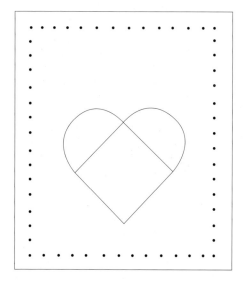

Use this template for the Amish Heart Notecard. Enlarge 200%, then 125%.

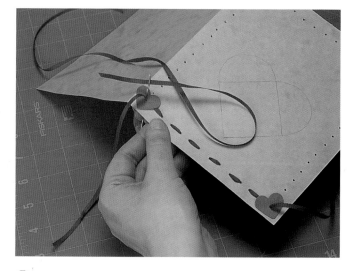

3 Lace the Ribbon Border

Pierce holes as marked along the front edges of the card using a tapestry needle, as in the previous step. Cut two 16" (40cm) pieces of red double-face satin-ribbon for the top and bottom edges of the card, and two 18" (45cm) pieces of ⅛" (3mm) wide red double-face satin ribbon for the sides of the card. Thread a tapestry needle with a piece of ribbon. Starting at a corner hole, thread on a heart button and sew a running stitch, bringing the needle under and over to complete each side. Thread on a button at each corner. The ribbon tails at each corner should be equal in length. Tie, seal and secure the bows at each corner.

4 | Weave the Center Square

Cut out the window opening, and then cut out and glue the paper semi-circles in place to create the heart shape. Weave the center square, using the technique described in step 3 of the bookmark project on page 86. For the woven square, you need four 4" (10cm) strips each of ⅝" (15mm) wide red and purple ribbon.

5 | Glue the Weaving and the Backing

Position the ribbon weaving behind the window and glue it in place, as for the bookmark in step 4, page 87. For a clean finish, cut a piece of lilac cardstock as a backing. Glue it over the back of the card front. You only need to glue around the edges of the backing card.

tip *You are investing your precious free time in making ribbon paper-crafts, so be sure to purchase acid-free, archival-quality papers and adhesives from craft or scrapbooking retailers. Remember to also inscribe the card using archival-quality inks.*

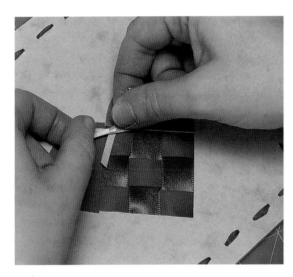

6 | Add a Contrasting Bow

Tie a bow using 8" (20cm) of pale lilac ribbon. Glue it onto the center top of the heart, using a dab of craft glue.

Apply this Amish patchwork heart to other paper gifts to show friends and family just how much you care.

Beaded Penny Rug Purse

This purse gives a pleasant update to a traditional

early-American needlecraft, the art of making

penny rugs. Concentric circles of felted wool, recycled

from old clothes, were blanket stitched onto background

fabric, and coins were used as circle templates.

Penny rugs were most often used as table coverings,

so their name is a bit misleading (penny mats

would be more accurate).

Ribbon

- 1$\frac{5}{8}$ yards (1.5m) of $\frac{1}{8}$" (31mm) wide blue double-face satin ribbon
- $\frac{3}{4}$ yard (60cm) of $\frac{1}{8}$" (3mm) wide forest green double-face satin ribbon
- $\frac{3}{8}$ yard (30cm) of green rat-tail cord
- 1$\frac{1}{8}$ yards (1m) of gold rat-tail cord
- 6$\frac{1}{2}$ yards (6m) of $\frac{1}{8}$" (3mm) wide golden yellow double-face satin ribbon

Supplies

- one 9"x12" (23 x 30cm) sheet of felt in each of the following colors: Cashmere Tan, Royal Blue and White (I used Kunin Rainbow Classic Felt)
- one package each of $\frac{1}{4}$" (5mm) frosted glass beads in golden yellow, royal blue and turquoise
- $\frac{1}{16}$" (1.6mm) circle hand punch
- tapestry needle and chenille needle
- needle and thread
- straight pins
- craft glue or liquid seam sealant
- tape measure

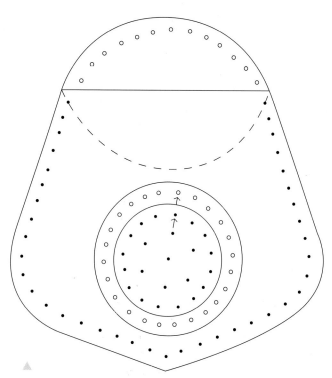

Use this template to make the Beaded Penny Rug Purse. Enlarge 200%.

1 Transfer the Template to the Felt

Transfer the pattern templates (purse front, purse back/flap, large circle and small circle) onto heavyweight paper. Tape the templates onto felt and cut them out in the colors shown. Punch holes in the felt with either a tapestry needle or the hand punch. Draw an arrow on each circle to mark your start position; you will then know when you have punched all the way around.

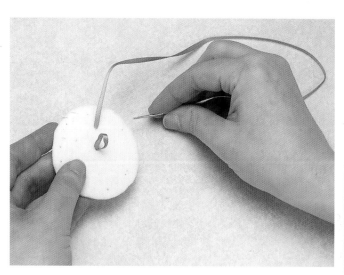

2 Begin Making a Lazy Daisy

The flower is made with a circle of ribbon-loop chain stitches. Thread a tapestry needle with 24" (60cm) of ¹/₈" (3mm) wide golden yellow ribbon. Bring the needle up at the circle center, make a loop, and bring the needle back down through the center hole. Bring the needle up at the hole directly above the loop.

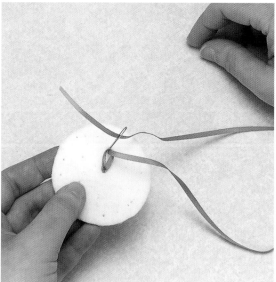

3 Complete the Petal

Pass the ribbon through the loop, then bring it back down the hole it last emerged from.

4 Finish the Daisy with a Center Bead

Work six petals to complete the daisy. Knot the ribbon on the wrong side and trim. Bring a new piece of ribbon through the center hole. Thread on a blue bead. Bring the ribbon back down and knot on the wrong side.

5 Start the Beaded Blanket Stitch

Center the white felt circle on the tan and baste in place. Thread a chenille needle with 24" (60cm) of green ribbon. Bring the needle up at any hole on the white circle. Thread on three turquoise beads. Bring the needle down through the next hole to the left. Bring the needle up, through both thicknesses of felt and through the lefthand side of the loop. Continue until the circle is fully beaded. Bring the needle through the last loop and knot the ribbon ends on the back.

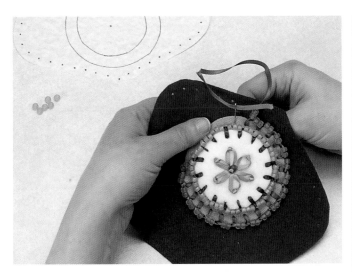

6 Bead the Front of the Purse

Center the two circles on the purse front and baste in place. Thread a chenille needle with 34" (86cm) of blue ribbon. Work the beaded blanket stitch all around the tan circle, this time threading only two gold beads on each blanket stitch (see page 21 for Beaded Blanket Stitch instructions).

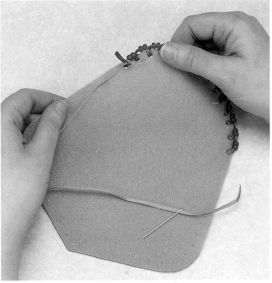

7 Stitch the Purse Flap

Thread a tapestry needle with 24" (60cm) of blue ribbon. Work a beaded blanket stitch only on the top portion of the purse back piece—this is the flap of the purse. Add two blue beads per stitch. Leave 2" (5cm) ribbon tails on each side of the stitching.

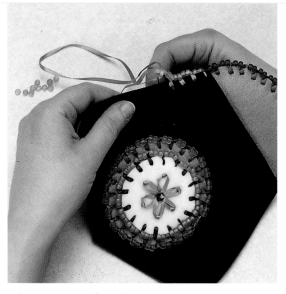

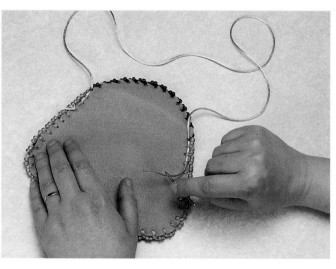

8 | Stitch the Purse Front to Back

Cut a 64" (1.6m) piece of golden yellow ribbon. Knot it onto the blue ribbon and trim the ribbon ends. The side with the knot is now the inside of the purse. With holes aligned, join the purse front to back using a beaded blanket stitch, two turquoise beads per stitch. Make sure the knot falls inside the purse when you finish stitching.

9 | Add the Shoulder Strap

Cut 38" (96cm) of silky gold cord. Seal the cord ends. Thread a tapestry needle with the cord. On the purse back, thread the cord through four stitch loops, then knot the cord end. Repeat for the other side.

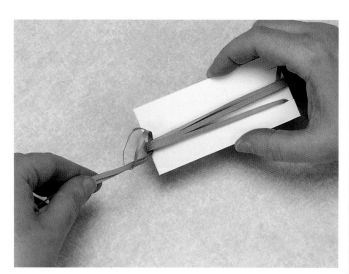

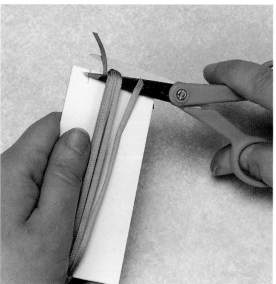

10 | Make the Tassel

Cut a piece of cardboard measuring 4" x 2" (10cm x 5cm). Cut two slits in one short end. Cut 140" (3.6m) of gold ribbon. Insert the ribbon end in the slit. Wrap the ribbon around the length of the card sixteen times, then insert the free end in the other slit. Cut a 10" (25cm) piece of ribbon. Loop it through the gold ribbon at the top of the card (opposite of the slits) and tie it tightly.

11 | Cut the Tassel

Cut across the bottom edge of the card to release the ribbon.

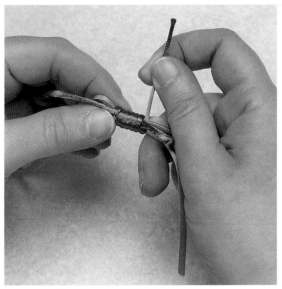

12 Wrap the Tassel Top

Secure the tassel by stitching through it with matching sewing thread. Knot the thread ends. Cut 10" (25cm) of green rat-tail cord. Next, wrap the tassel top. First, loop the cord, then hold the loop in place on the tassel, loop downward.

13 Attach the Tassel to the Purse

Wrap the cord around the tassel top downward. When you reach the bottom, thread the cord through the loop. Trim the cord so only about $^3/_4$" (2cm) extends. Slowly tug on the cord at the tassel top to conceal the tail. Tie the tassel onto the loop at the bottom point of the purse back. Trim the ribbon close to the knot and seal the ribbon ends with glue.

variation idea

The finished Beaded Penny Rug Purse makes a fashionable addition to any wardrobe!

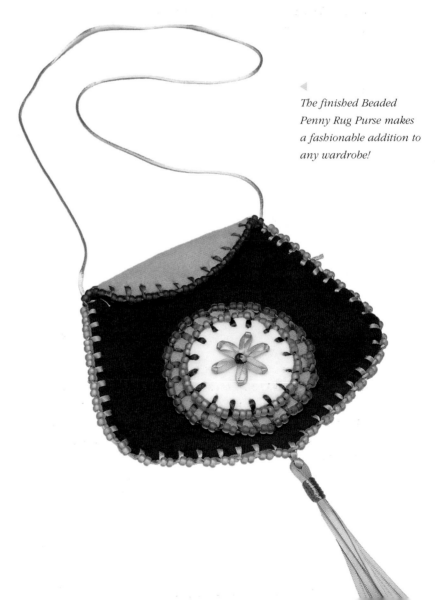

Try this as an alternative to the beaded purse. You'll need 2$^1/_2$ yards (2.3m) of narrow $^1/_8$" (3mm) wide ribbon for the blanket stitching around the outside edges, and twice as much ribbon for the double tassels. Use a jumbo bead to hold the flap shut.

Rose Garland Makeup Bag

Roses are just about the easiest ribbon flowers you

can make. Their simplicity does not make them any less

impressive, though. If you can sew a ribbon loop, then

you are well on your way to making these delightful

blooms. Using a sewing machine speeds things up, but

you can make them entirely by hand if you choose.

This duffel-style makeup pouch is pretty and practical,

with a vinyl lining to protect against spills.

Ribbon

- $^3/_4$ yard (60cm) of $^7/_8$" (23mm) wide apricot double-face satin ribbon
- $^1/_4$ yard (20cm) of $^5/_8$" (15mm) wide apricot double-face satin ribbon
- $^3/_4$ yard (60cm) of $^7/_8$" (23mm) wide lilac double-face satin ribbon
- $1^3/_8$ yards (1.2m) of $^5/_8$" (15mm) wide lilac double-face satin ribbon
- $^7/_8$ yard (80cm) of $^1/_4$" (7mm) wide mint green double-face satin ribbon
- $1^3/_8$ yards (1.2m) of $^3/_8$" (9mm) wide mint green double-face satin ribbon

Supplies

- $^1/_2$ yard (40cm) of cream satin fabric
- $^3/_8$ yard (30cm) of frosted or clear vinyl
- 10 pearl beads
- 2 cream plastic hairbeads
- needle and thread
- straight pins
- fabric glue or liquid seam sealant
- tape measure

SEWING MACHINE REQUIRED

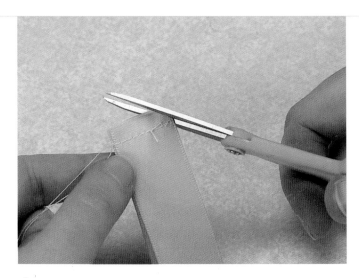

1 Begin the Rose

Cut a 6" (15cm) length of 7/8" (23mm) wide apricot or lilac ribbon. Seal the ribbon ends with craft glue. Stitch the short ends together to form a loop, using a 1/4" (7mm) seam allowance. You can sew the seam either by hand or machine. Knot the thread ends and sew in the tails with a sewing needle. Trim the bottom of the seam diagonally. Seal the newly cut edges.

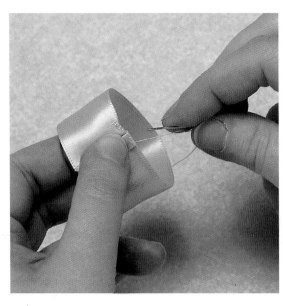

2 Stitch the Seam Allowance

Finger-press the seam open. Stitch the top edges of the seam allowances to the ribbon loop, so they lie flat.

3 Gather the Top of the Loop

Using doubled sewing thread, hand-sew a running stitch around the top of the loop. Use fairly large stitches. Begin and end at the loop seam. Gently pull up the gathers and knot the thread. For the makeup bag bottom border, make four apricot and four lilac roses.

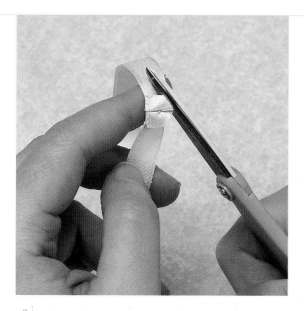

4 Begin the Double-Leaf

The double-leaf begins with a ribbon loop, just like the rose. Cut a 6" (15cm) strip of ³/₈" (9mm) wide mint green ribbon. Follow steps 1 and 2 for making the leaf loop. Finger-press the leaf loop flat, so the seam falls at the loop's midpoint. Baste the long edges of the loop together on one side of the flattened loop—the side where the seam allowances are stitched down.

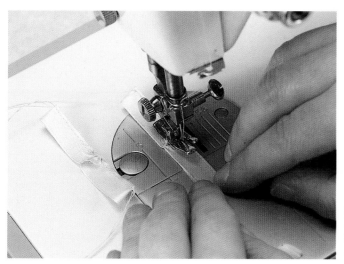

5 Sew the Long Edges

Seam the loop together, stitching very close to the edge. You can do this by machine or hand. Knot the thread ends, but do not cut them off.

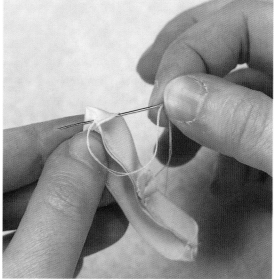

6 Turn the Leaf Tips to the Right Side

Spread open the seam and turn the ends to the right side. Use a needle to pick out a nice crisp point. On the wrong side of the leaves, thread a needle with thread ends. Sew the ribbon onto the seam at either end.

7 | Gather the Center of the Double-Leaf

Thread a needle with doubled sewing thread. Take three stitches across the center of the double-leaf—under, over, under, as shown.

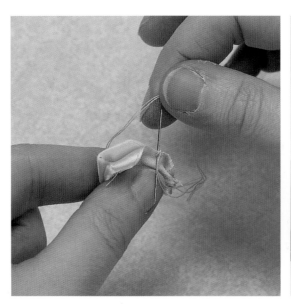

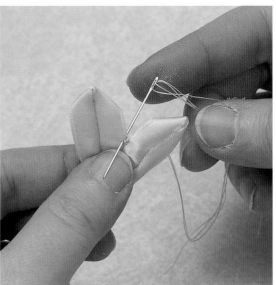

8 | Stitch the Leaves Together

Pull up the gathers, then knot them on the wrong side of the double-leaf. Do not cut the thread. With right sides together, fold the leaves in half. Thread a needle with doubled thread and make several stitches through the folded edges of both layers, stitching upward from the leaf center.

9 | Open the Double-Leaf

Unfold the double-leaf. On the right side, make several stitches at the top end of the seam. Knot the thread on the back and cut it off. Make a total of eight leaves in this way.

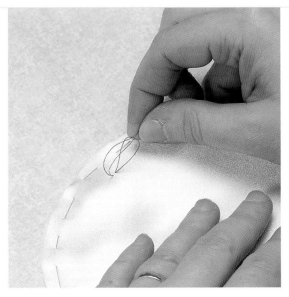

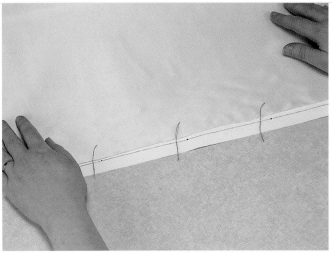

10 Cut Out the Base of the Bag

From the satin, cut out a circular bag base 6½" (17cm) in diameter. From the vinyl, cut out another circle the same size. Pin the vinyl circle to the matte side of the satin with edges matching. Baste around the edges of the vinyl, through both layers. Make tailor's tacks (see page 18) at the 12, 3, 6, and 9 o'clock positions on the circular bag base, ⅝" (1.5cm) from the edge. These will correspond with the body of the bag.

11 Measure and Cut the Body of the Bag

Cut a 15" x 18½" (39cm x 47cm) piece of satin. Then cut a 11" x 18½" (28cm x 47cm) rectangle of vinyl. Mark a ⅝" (1.5cm) seam allowance all around the body of the bag, then space tailor's tacks at 4¼" (11cm) intervals along the bottom seam allowance. The tailor's tacks divide the base of the bag into quarters, not including the side seam allowances.

12 Sew the Bag

With the matte sides of the satin facing each other, pin the short sides of the bag rectangle together. Notice that the satin extends above the vinyl. Stitch a seam, with a ⅝" (1.5cm) allowance. This forms the tube that is the body of the makeup bag. Turn the bag to the right side.

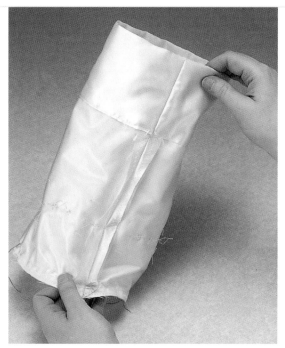

13 | Create a Finished Top Edge

Turn under the top edge of bag ⁵/₈" (1.5cm). Spread open and flatten the seam allowance of the bag side seam before you turn the top edge under. Baste down the folded edge. Fold the top of the bag body under 3¹/₂" (9cm), along the edge of the vinyl lining. Baste down the bottom edge of the turning, then machine-stitch it close to the edge. You now have a tube with a finished top edge.

14 | Add the Roses

Pin the flower garland 1¹/₂" (4cm) above the bag base. Start with a flower centered at the back seam. Alternate apricot and lilac flowers, with double-leaves in between. There are eight flowers and eight double-leaves in total. Sew a pearl bead to the center of each flower, catching in all layers (rose and bag). Stitch the flower garland down using matching sewing thread. Sew on the leaves at the leaf tips and center, and the flowers at opposite sides. To finish the body of the bag, turn the bag inside out and stitch all around the base ¹/₂" (12mm) from the edge. Cut the fabric close to the stitching at regularly-spaced intervals. With the right sides together, pin the bag base to the bag body, matching tailor's tacks. Baste in place, then stitch the bag base to the body using a ⁵/₈" (1.5cm) seam allowance.

15 | Add the Drawstring Loops

Cut four 6" (15cm) pieces of ¹/₄" (7mm) wide mint green satin ribbon. Fold the ribbon in half and knot 1" (2.5cm) below the loop. Trim the angled tails 1" (2.5cm) below the knot. Seal the ribbon ends. Repeat for the three remaining ribbon pieces. Hand-sew four equally spaced drawstring loops onto the right side of the makeup bag, along the horizontal stitching line around the bag. Place the first loop at the back seam. Sew on each loop through the knot.

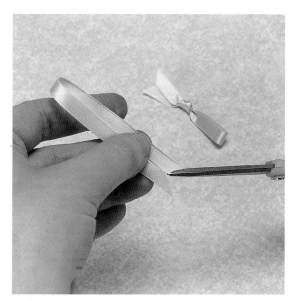

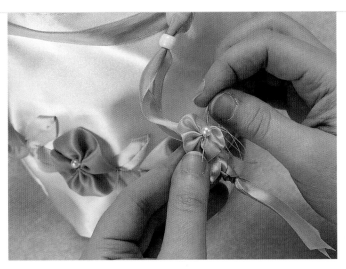

16 Add the Drawstring

Cut two 24" (60cm) pieces of lilac ribbon for the drawstring. Angle and seal the ends. Thread the ribbon through the carriers, one piece on each side of the bag. Thread on a bead at both sides of the drawstring, over the doubled ribbons. Knot each side of the drawstring about 2" (5cm) from the end. Make two mini-roses and double-leaves. Sew a rose and leaf onto each side of the drawstring, near the knot. Each mini-rose requires 4" (10cm) of 5/8" (15mm) wide ribbon. (Take a 1/4" [7mm] seam when making the loops.)

variation idea

Once you start making rose garlands, it is difficult to stop. Why not make an entire bedroom ensemble? Pillowcases, sheets, night-gowns, slippers—almost anything can be decorated. The roses look especially delicate when you make them in graduated sizes. Simply vary the width of the ribbon and the length of the strips. You can also sew on the garlands in curved or circular arrangements.

▲

Fill this elegant bag with your favorite cosmetics, or give it as a gift for someone special.

wedding and baby

Weddings and births are the two happiest events of a lifetime...

and what better way to celebrate than with ribboncraft projects? Handmade wedding accessories have more character than their mass-produced counterparts. You have taken the time to create unique mementos, and both the time spent crafting and the objects themselves will be valued by the bride and groom.

The wedding projects in this section share a rose trellis theme. Ribbon roses, both purchased and handmade, pearl beads, sheer ribbons and brocades all contribute to the opulent total effect. There are projects for the bride, the ceremony, the reception and for preserving cherished memories. Projects include a ring bearer's pillow, a basket for confetti, and memory boxes that resemble a tiered wedding cake.

The birth of a baby is another milestone, and a heartfelt way to celebrate the miraculous occasion is to welcome the new arrival. A ribbon-trimmed baby blanket is a quick makeover for a store bought fleece blanket. The nursery mobile made out of an embroidery hoop, ribbons and pearlescent cardboard will fascinate and delight the baby.

Ribboncraft is not only a way to embellish ordinary days. It is also a fabulous way to mark special occasions. You will enjoy creating these projects and celebrating life's wonderful moments!

Projects

Wedding Cake Memory Boxes

A wedding is the event of a lifetime. Cherished wedding

memorabilia merits a very special home of its own. These

tiered "wedding cake" boxes store treasured wedding

keepsakes in style. The biggest boxes are spacious enough

to hold items such as the bridal veil, while the smaller

containers are just right for snapshots, cards and other

keepsakes. Organize these precious memories by writing

the contents of each box on the heart-shaped index tags.

Ribbon

- 2⅝ yards (4cm) of 1½" (39mm) wide lilac double-face lilac satin ribbon
- 1⅜ yards (1.2m) of ⅛" (3mm) wide lilac satin ribbon
- ⅝ yard (50cm) of ⅛" (3mm) wide moss green satin ribbon
- 8 yards (7.2m) of ⅛" (3mm) wide white satin ribbon
- 1⅜ yards (1.2m) of ⅝" (15mm) wide white sheer-stripe ribbon
- 1⅜ yards (1.2m) of ⅛" (3mm) wide lilac satin ribbon
- ½ yard (50cm) of ⅝" (15mm) wide lilac double-face satin ribbon
- ⅜ yard (30cm) of 1" (25mm) wide bridal white sheer stripe ribbon
- ⅜ yard (30cm) of 1" (25mm) wide bridal white satin ribbon
- 55 lilac satin rosebuds

Supplies

- 4 round pâpier-mâché boxes, in graduated sizes in the following diameters: 10" (25cm), 8" (20cm), 5¼" (13cm) and 4" (10cm)
- lilac cardstock
- off-white handmade paper giftwrap
- 4½ yards (4.2m) of pearl beading
- 1 pack of 3/16" (4mm) diameter pearl beads
- off-white acrylic paint and paintbrush
- 1/16" (1.6mm) circle hand punch
- tapestry needle
- needle and thread
- craft glue
- gluestick
- tape measure

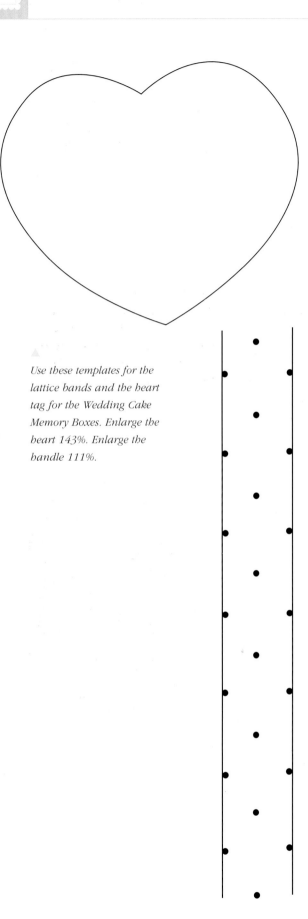

Use these templates for the lattice bands and the heart tag for the Wedding Cake Memory Boxes. Enlarge the heart 143%. Enlarge the handle 111%.

1 | Paint the Box and Lid

Paint the box and the lids with off-white acrylic paint to cover up the brown pâpier-mâché color. A second coat may be needed.

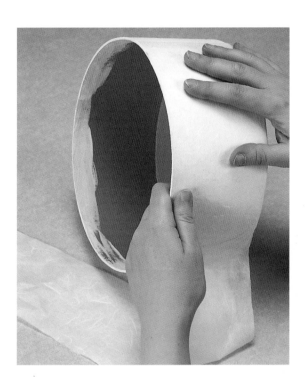

2 | Cover the Box with Giftwrap

Trace around the lid onto the back of the handmade gift wrap and cut out the circle. For the lid side pattern, cut a strip ³/₄" (2cm) longer than the box's circumference and ¹/₈" (3mm) wider than the lid's height. Cut a piece of gift wrap for the box base. Measure it in the same way as for the lid. Apply the glue stick to the wrong side of the handmade paper. Smooth the circle onto the box top. Apply the side strip by aligning the paper overlap with the seam in the lid.

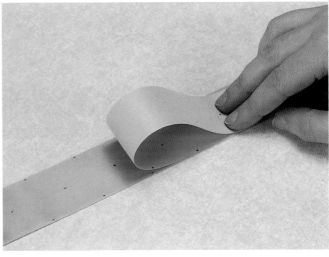

3 Make a Guide for the Lattice Bands

Copy the pattern on page 108 onto a piece of stiff paper. Cut out a paper strip to size, mark dots along sides and punch center holes as marked.

4 Transfer the Lattice Design Onto the Ribbon

For each box, cut a band of 1¹/₂"(39mm) wide lilac ribbon measuring 2¹/₂" (6cm) longer than the box circumference. Seal the ribbon ends with glue. Carefully transfer the lattice design onto the lilac ribbon. You will use this as a guide to keep your latticework consistent and even. The dots on the lilac ribbon show you where to place the narrow ribbon in order to create the criss-cross design.

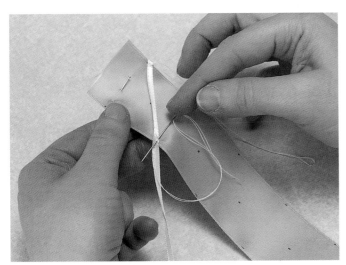

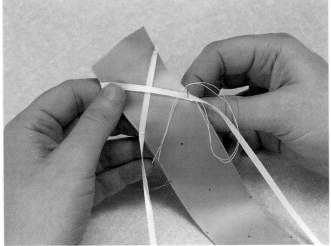

5 Begin Stitching on the Lattice

Cut a piece of ¹/₈" (3mm) wide white ribbon three times the length of the lilac band. Fold the white ribbon in half, and pin the folded end behind the lilac ribbon, close to one end. Fold the narrow ribbon diagonally, right to left, matching dots. Sew the ribbon to the lilac ribbon at the dots with matching thread.

6 Fold the Opposite Diagonal

Cross the ribbon over, from left to right. Sew at the markings, just as in the previous step.

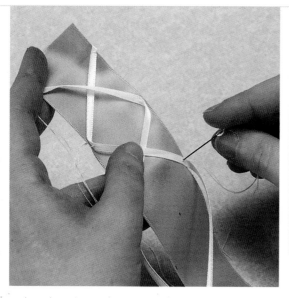

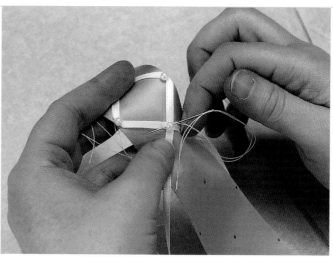

7 Continue Making the Lattice Design

Pick up the righthand ribbon and fold it to the left. Sew as shown. Repeat with the lefthand ribbon, and continue the design all the way down the lilac ribbon.

8 Sew on the Pearl Beads

Sew on pearl beads at all the diamond points. Leave the last inch or two on one end of the band unbeaded for the underlap. Mark a line on the box about 1/2" (1cm) above the box bottom.

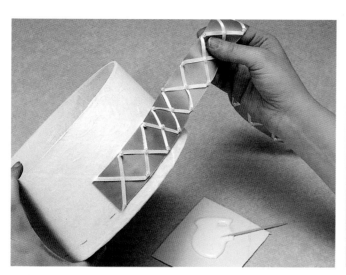

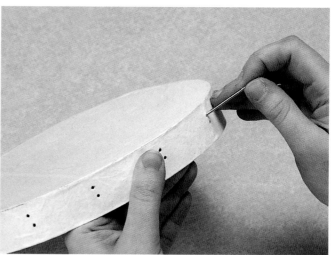

9 Glue the Lattice to the Boxes

Glue the lattice band onto the box at the marked level, starting with the bead-free end. Align the short end of the band with the giftwrap seam on the box. Apply craft glue onto wrong side of the ribbon. Glue a small portion at a time.

tip It is a good idea to test-glue the lilac ribbon before making the lattice band. If glue soaks through, you'll need to interface the ribbon. (See the Nosegay Towel project, page 32, steps 1 and 2.)

10 Measure the Lid for the Beading

Measure the lid circumference and divide it into equal segments of about 2" (5cm). Mark around the lid, 1/4" (7mm) below the lid top and 2" (5cm) apart. Mark a second dot 1/4" (7mm) below each one. Use a tapestry needle to pierce holes at the marked dots. The pâpier-mâché is soft and easily pierced.

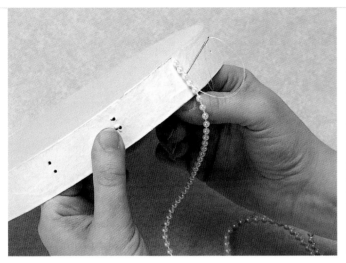

11 | Attach the Beading

Cut the beading to the required length. For the smallest box, you need 2¹⁄₂" (6.5cm) of beading per segment. For all other box sizes, you need 3¹⁄₄" (8.5cm) per segment. (Multiply the segment length by the number of segments to get the total length of beading.) Pre-measure the beading segments and tie on a piece of doubled thread to mark each one. You can then thread the needle and sew on the beading segment by segment.

12 | Add the Beading and Roses

Sew through the double holes. Knot the thread inside the lid. Repeat for the other segments to form the swags. You may want to sew the ribbon roses at the same time as the beading with one stitch. Combining the two steps saves time. Stitch through the rose center.

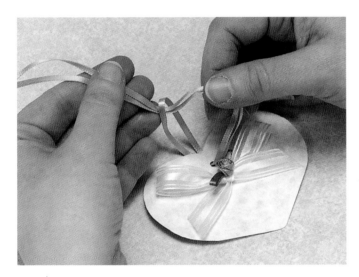

13 | Make the Index Tags

The pattern for the tag is given on page 108. Cut a heart out of lilac card-stock and pierce a hole at the top. Glue on a bow made from 12" (30cm) of sheer stripe ⁵⁄₈" (15mm) wide ribbon. Glue on a ribbon rosebud, and loop a tie through the top hole. For each tie, you need 12" (30cm) of ¹⁄₈" (3mm) wide lilac satin ribbon. To attach the tag, tie it through a beaded swag.

14 | **Seam the Satin Ribbon**

Cut 12" (30cm) lengths each of the 1" (25mm) sheer stripe and the 1" (25mm) white satin ribbon. Overlap and baste along one long edge. Machine-stitch close to the edge to make a double-width ribbon.

15 | **Gather the Satin Ribbon**

Seam the short ends of the ribbon, then gather the top edge (see the Nosegay Towel project, pages 33-34, steps 8 and 9 for detailed instructions). Pull up the gathers, and knot on the wrong side.

16 | **Sew on the Ribbon Rose**

Make a lilac ribbon rose (see the Ring Bearer's Pillow on pages 118-119, steps 9-14). Sew the rose onto the satin ribbon center. Finally, glue the rose onto the lid of the smallest box, using craft glue.

variation idea

Custom-decorate the flower girl's footwear. Sew rosettes onto plain satin wedding shoes. Follow steps 14–16 to make the roses. The length of the ribbon pieces should be 10¹/₂" (26cm). Sew on rosebud-trimmed sheer ribbon bows at the heels. She'll look sweet going up the aisle.

Stack all four nested boxes on top of one another to create a tiered wedding cake centerpiece.

Ring Bearer's Pillow

A woven-ribbon heart, a romantic symbol of two lives

intertwined, is the motif for this exquisite ring pillow.

Designed with the occasion in mind, the pillow's bow

streamers will flutter gracefully as it is paraded up the

aisle. The woven heart is an ideal introduction to the

craft of ribbon weaving. The heart is constructed with

both satin and brocade ribbons in a variety of sizes and

outlined with a braided border of satin ribbons.

Ribbon

- $1/2$ yard (40cm) of $5/8$" (15mm) wide lilac double-face satin ribbon
- 1 yard (90cm) of $3/8$" (9mm) wide lilac double-face satin ribbon
- $2^3/8$ yards (2.2m) of $1/8$" (3mm) wide lilac double-face satin ribbon
- $1^1/2$ yards (1.3m) of $1/8$" (3mm) wide moss green double-face satin ribbon
- $2^1/2$ yards (2.3m) each of 1" (25mm), $5/8$" (15mm) and $3/8$" (9mm) wide bridal white double-face satin ribbon
- 2 yards (1.8m) of $1/8$" (3mm) wide white double-face satin ribbon
- $2^1/2$ yards (2.3m) each of 1" (25mm), $5/8$" (15mm), and $3/8$" (9mm) wide bridal white brocade ribbon
- $4^7/8$ yards (4.5m) of $3/4$" (20mm) wide bridal white sheer stripe ribbon

Supplies

- $3/8$ yard (30cm) off-white satin fabric
- $3/8$ yard (30cm) of 12 oz. (340g) polyester batting or one 10" (25cm) square pillow form
- 12" (30cm) of lightweight iron-on interfacing
- needle and thread
- straight pins
- fabric glue or liquid seam sealant
- tape measure
- press cloth
- toothpick

SEWING MACHINE REQUIRED

*Use this heart template for
the Ring Bearer Pillow.
Enlarge 143%.*

1 | Begin the Ribbon Weave

For an easy method of ribbon weaving, pin the ribbons directly onto your ironing board. Cut a 9" (23cm) square of iron-on interfacing and place it adhesive side-up on the ironing board. Cut the plain and brocade ribbons into 10" (25cm) strips. To make up the vertical threads of the weaving, pin the ribbons side by side, alternating each one. Completely cover the interfacing using three or four strips of each ribbon type and width. Pin the ribbons at the top and bottom, angling the pins away from the ribbons.

2 | Weave the Ribbon

Weave the horizontal ribbons through the vertical ribbons. Make sure the ribbons are flush with each other and at right angles to the vertical ribbons. Pin the ribbon ends. Press the ribbon weaving with a dry iron on a medium setting. Use a press cloth or a handkerchief to protect the ribbons.

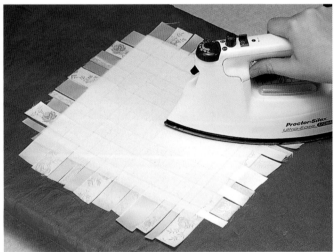

3 | Press the Wrong Side

Remove all of the pins and flip the weaving onto the wrong side. Iron the interfacing according to the manufacturer's instructions to fuse the bond.

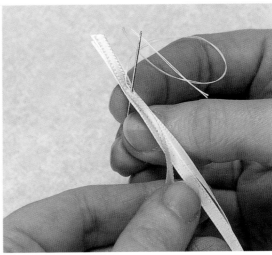

4 Cut Out the Heart Shape

Enlarge the heart template from page 116, so the length of the heart measures 6" (15cm) tall. Pin it onto the weaving and make an outline stitch around the shape in contrasting thread. With a sewing machine, zigzag around the outline. Next, cut out the woven heart, just outside the zigzag stitching. (If you do not have a zigzag sewing machine, a straight stitch or hand-sewn back stitch will do.)

5 Begin the Braid

Cut two 1-yard (90cm) pieces of ⅛" (3mm) wide white ribbon, and one piece of lilac ribbon the same length. Stack the ends one on top of the other, sandwiching the lilac in between the white. Stitch through all the layers at the end to anchor the ribbons. This produces a flat, knot-free start to the braid.

tip When making a three-strand braid, the length of each strand of ribbon must be about one and a half times the desired finished length of the braid.

7 Sew the Braid Around the Heart

Starting and finishing at the heart "valley," hand stitch the braid around heart, concealing the machine zigzags. Use matching sewing thread, and try to hide your stitches.

6 Braid the Ribbon

Braid the three pieces of ribbon, keeping the ribbon flat at all times. Continue braiding until you have a braid 21" (52cm) long, then stitch the ribbon ends together, just as you did at the braid's beginning.

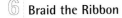

8 Sew on a Bow

Make a bow from 15" (38cm) of ³/₄" (20mm) wide sheer-stripe ribbon. Trim the ribbon ends, then seal them with fabric glue. Pin and then sew the bow onto the pillow.

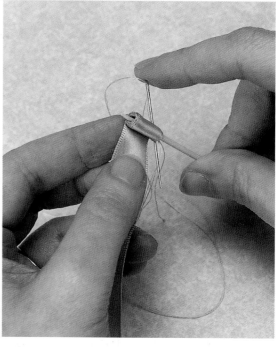

9 Start the Ribbon Rose

For the large ribbon rose at the top of the heart, cut 16" (40cm) of ⁵/₈" (15mm) wide lilac ribbon. Seal the ribbon ends. Start the rose by twirling the ribbon counterclockwise around a toothpick to make a tight coil—the rosebud. Add a few stitches at the base of the coil to secure it. Remove the toothpick after the coil is stitched.

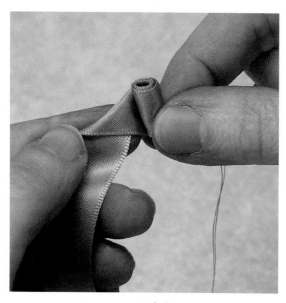

10 Form a Rose Petal

Fold the ribbon diagonally downward as you continue spiralling counterclockwise. This creates a rose petal.

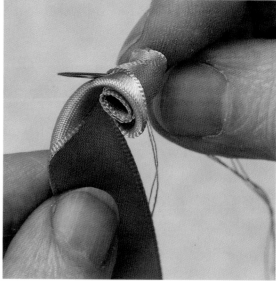

11 Secure Each Fold with a Stitch

As you roll the ribbon around the coil, stitch the ribbon to the coil at the bottom cross-point of each fold. The rosebud should not extend above the height of the petals.

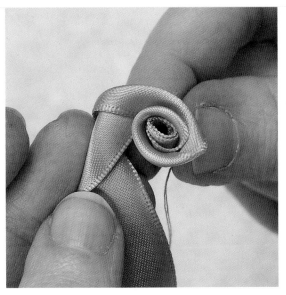

12 Continue Spiralling and Stitching

Fold, roll and stitch the ribbon to build up the rose. You can control the look of your rose by coiling loosely or tightly. This rose has a wide open appearance. For a more compact rose, coil with a tighter tension.

13 Finish the Rose

Continue spiralling until the ribbon ends, then fold the ribbon end under diagonally and stitch it down.

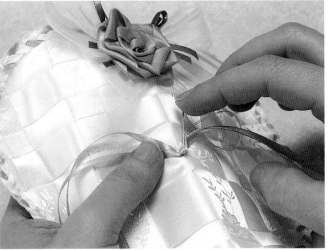

14 Sew the Rose Onto the Heart

Cut two 10" (25cm) pieces of moss green ribbon to make a double bow for the rose "leaves." Stack the ribbons and tie the bow, treating the two ribbons as one. Trim and seal the bow ends. Pin the bow, then the rose, onto the large white bow. Stitch through all of the layers at the heart "valley."

15 Sew on the Ring Ties

Cut two 25" (64cm) pieces of 1/8" (3mm) wide lilac ribbon. Place one piece on top of the other and knot at the center. Sew the knot onto the center of the woven heart.

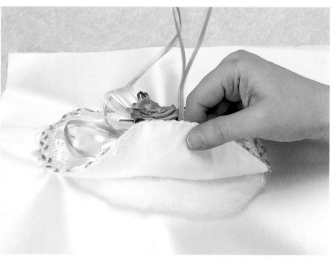

16 Stitch the Batting

Cut three 10" (25cm) squares from the batting. Stack them on top of each other and baste close to the edges. Stitch all around the edges to complete the pillow form. Remove the basting. You may also use a pre-made pillow form.

17 Hand-Stitch the Heart in Place

Cut out two pieces of lightweight interfacing 11¼" x 11¼" (28cm x 28cm). Bond each piece of interfacing onto the matte side of a piece of satin, following the manufacturer's instructions. Trim the satin to the exact size of the interfacing squares. Pin the heart onto the pillow front. Hand-sew the heart onto the pillow front using matching sewing thread.

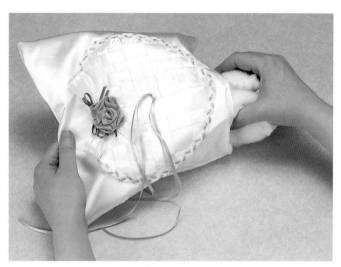

18 Sew and Stuff the Pillow

Pin the pillow front to the back, right sides together. Machine stitch around the pillow, using a ⅝" (1.5cm) seam allowance. Leave about 6½" (17cm) unstitched on one side. Turn the pillow right side out and insert the pillow form. Baste the opening shut, then slip stitch it into place. (To review Slip Stitch instructions, see page 21.)

19 Sew on the Corner Bows

Cut four pieces of sheer-stripe ribbon, each 40" (1m) long. Tie each into a bow, trim the ribbon ends and seal them. Cut four pieces of ⅜" (9mm) wide lilac ribbon, each measuring 8" (20cm) long, and four pieces of ⅛" (3mm) moss green ribbon, each also 8" (20cm) long. Make four lilac ribbon roses and four leaf bows, repeating steps 9-14. Pin a white bow, a green bow and a rose onto each corner, ¾" (2cm) from the tip. Sew them onto the pillow through all the layers.

variation ideas

You can customize a purchased archival-quality scrapbook with the same rose trellis theme. Start with a moiré-covered album, about 12" (30cm) square. Make a woven heart appliqué (see above) and two lattice bands (see Wedding Cake Memory Boxes, page 107). Glue them onto the album cover. Cover the album with a piece of tracing paper, then weight the album with books as it dries.

Make a bridal purse by decorating an envelope of brocade fabric with a mini woven heart and a lattice band (see Wedding Cake Memory Boxes, page 107). For the shoulder strap, sew on pearl beading. To attach the beading, stitch it down at bag's side seams, catching the beading between beads. Add decorative bows to conceal the stitching. You can also use these techniques to dress up a storebought purse.

Use this precious Ring Bearer's Pillow as a keepsake to remember your special day.

Wedding Reception Papercrafts

After the ceremony, celebrate your marriage with a

personalized wedding reception. The Confetti Basket is a

beautiful alternative to throwing rice, and the Favor

Pillow Box is perfect for holding sweet treats. You can

also impress your guests with the Rose Trellis Menu Card.

Although elegant in appearance, this hand-made holder

for the menu doesn't take long to make. Inside the card,

glue a copy of the wedding dinner menu.

1 Confetti Basket • *page 124*

Ribbon

- 2¼ yards (2.1m) of ⅛" (3mm) wide lilac double-face satin ribbon
- 8 lilac ribbon rosebuds

Supplies

- ⅜ yard (30cm) of white tulle
- lilac parchment-look cardstock
- ¹/₁₆" (1.6mm) circle hand punch
- craft knife and cutting mat
- tapestry needle
- needle and thread
- craft glue
- confetti

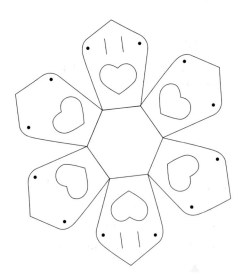

Use these templates for the Confetti Basket and Handle. Enlarge each 222%.

1 Cut Out the Paper Basket

With the templates provided, cut out the basket and handle. Use a craft knife and ruler for straight lines, small scissors for the curves, and a hand punch to make the holes at the marked dots. If you don't own a hand punch, pierce the holes with a tapestry needle. Remember to cut slits for the basket handles.

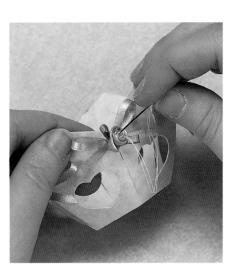

2 Connect the Sides of the Basket

Cut six 8" (20cm) pieces of lilac ribbon for the ties. Thread a ribbon through the adjacent basket sides—a tapestry needle can help to get the ribbon through the holes. Tie a bow, trim the ribbon ends and seal with craft glue. Add a ribbon rosebud over the bow knot, sewing through all layers. Repeat for the remaining five sides.

3 Make the Lattice Design

Cut a 20" (50cm) piece of ribbon. Knot one end and thread it through the hole at the end of the handle. Evenly wrap the ribbon around the handle, spiralling upward. Thread the ribbon through the hole at the opposite end of the handle. Make sure both knots lie on the same side of the handle. Attach the handle to the basket and set a tulle pouch filled with confetti inside.

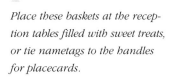

Place these baskets at the reception tables filled with sweet treats, or tie nametags to the handles for placecards.

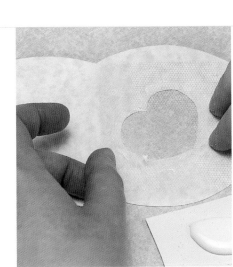

2 Favor Pillow Box

Ribbon

- ⁵/₈ yard (50cm) of ¹/₈" (3mm) wide lilac double-face satin ribbon
- 1 lilac ribbon rosebud

Supplies

- 4" (10cm) square of tulle
- lilac parchment-look cardstock
- deep lilac pearlescent paper
- ¹/₂" (12mm) heart-shaped paper punch
- craft knife and cutting mat
- needle and thread
- craft glue

1 Cut Out the Box and Glue the Tulle

Use the template below to cut out a pillow box form. On the right side of the box, lightly score the curved flaps and the long straight folds. Cut a square of tulle measuring 2¹/₄" (6cm). On the wrong side, apply glue around the edge of the heart-shaped window. Glue the tulle behind the window, smoothing it into place.

2 Glue the Box Together

Crease the box along the straight scored lines. Apply glue to the long flap, then glue down the back of the box.

Fill this box with sugared almonds or other sweets for your guests at the reception.

3 Embellish the Box

Punch out two hearts from pearlescent paper. Glue them onto the box front, as shown. On one side, fold under the back flap, then the front flap. Fill the box with candy, then close the remaining two flaps in the same order. Cut a 20" (50cm) piece of ribbon and wrap it around the box. Tie a bow at the top left corner and sew on a ribbon rosebud.

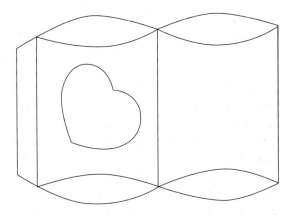

Use this template for the Favor Pillow Box. Enlarge 182%.

3 Menu Card

Ribbon

- ½ yard (40cm) of ⅜" (3mm) wide lilac double-face satin ribbon
- 1¼ yards (1.1m) of ⅛" (3mm) wide lilac double-face satin ribbon
- 1 yard (80cm) of ⅛" (3mm) wide moss green double-face satin ribbon

Supplies

- lilac parchment-look cardstock
- white parchment-look paper
- 26 white pearl beads
- 1/16" (1.6mm) circle hand punch
- craft knife and cutting mat
- tapestry needle
- needle and thread
- craft glue
- glue stick
- metal ruler

1 Cut Out the Menu Card

Fold each side of the lilac cardstock in toward the center of the paper, so that the edges are touching one another. Your paper should now have a left and a right flap, resembling double doors. Using the template below, match the center line of the cardstock with the center line of the template. Cut out the menu card, score the folds and punch holes at the marked dots.

NOTE: *For multiple cards, make a template out of heavy cardstock or cardboard.*

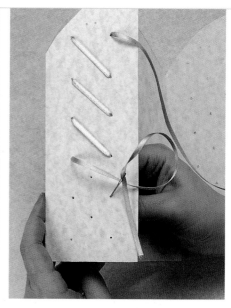

2 Begin to Lace the Lattice

Cut two pieces of ⅛" wide lilac ribbon, each measuring 21" (52cm) long. Thread the ribbon with a tapestry needle and lace through the two top trellis holes with roughly half the ribbon on each side. The closely spaced holes at the very top of the card are for attaching the roses; the trellis holes are below them. Stitch the first left-to-right diagonal. Progress from top to bottom, lacing all the lefthand diagonal stitches.

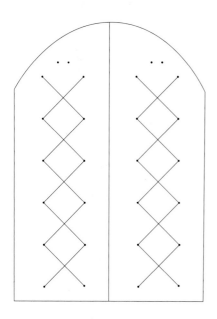

Use this template for the Menu Card. Enlarge 200%, then 143%.

3 Complete the Lattice Crosses

To complete the lattice, re-thread the needle with the remaining ribbon on the righthand side. Lace all the right-to-left diagonals, completing the crosses.

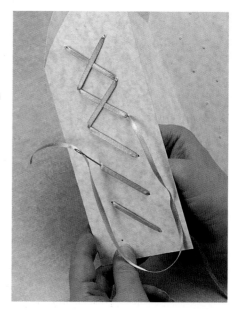

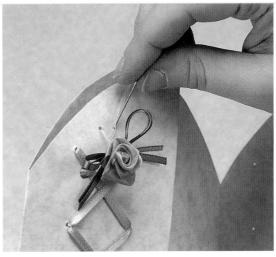

4 Tie Off the Ribbon

Tie a knot at the bottom of the card. Trim the ribbon tails close to the knot. Lace the other side of the card in the same way.

5 Add a Ribbon Rose

For each ribbon rose, you need 8" (20cm) of $^3/_8$" (9mm) lilac ribbon, and two 8" (20cm) pieces of moss green ribbon. Make two ribbon roses, following steps 9–14 for the Ring Bearer's Pillow on page 114. Sew each ribbon rose onto the front of the card, using the lacing holes provided.

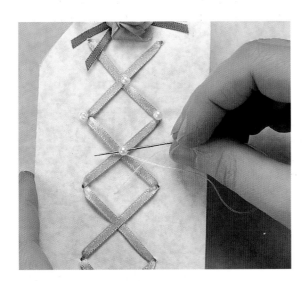

6 Add the Final Touches

Using doubled white thread, sew on a pearl bead at the diamond corners. Ad beads at the bottom end of the lattice if you wish. Knot the thread on the card back. Conceal the ribbon work on the back of each flap with a piece of white paper, cut to fit. You only need to glue it around the edges. Last but not least, glue a menu onto the card interior center panel of the card.

Write out the wedding menu in calligraphy. Or, hand-letter the original photocopying the rest.

Nursery Carousel

This fantasy confection of pastel ribbons and bows

makes a delightful addition to any child's room.

It is also very economical to make—this mobile

consists of a wooden embroidery hoop, ribbon and

paper. It makes a great baby shower gift for a boy or

girl. The new baby will be mesmerized watching the

chicks on the carousel go 'round and 'round.

Ribbon

- $2^7/_8$ yards (2.6m) of $^1/_4$" (7mm) wide blue satin ribbon
- $^7/_8$ yard (80cm) of $^1/_4$" (7mm) wide pink satin ribbon
- $^7/_8$ yard (80cm) of 1" (25mm) wide blue sheer ribbon (such as polyester organdy)
- $^7/_8$ yard (80cm) of $1^1/_2$" (39mm) wide yellow sheer ribbon (such as polyester organdy)
- $1^3/_4$ yards (1.6m) each of $^1/_8$" (3mm) wide double-face satin ribbon in yellow, lilac, pink and blue satin

Supplies

- yellow, lilac, pink and blue pearlescent cardstock
- yellow, purple, pink and blue paper
- 12" (30cm) diameter wooden embroidery hoop
- 1" (2.5cm) diameter plastic curtain ring
- 1 large-holed frosted plastic bead, about 1" (2.5cm) in diameter
- pastel yellow acrylic craft paint and paintbrush
- $^1/_4$" (7mm) and $^1/_{16}$" (1.6mm) circle hand punches
- craft knife and cutting mat
- tapestry needle
- needle and thread
- straight pins
- craft glue
- glue stick
- tape measure

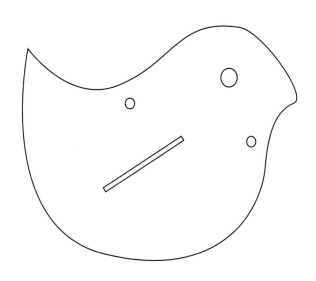

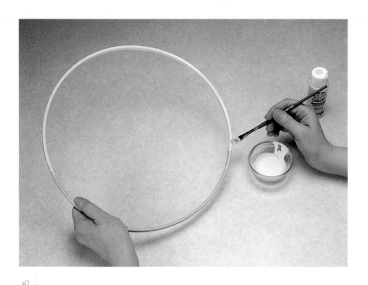

Use this template for the Nursery
Carousel. Enlarge 125%.

1 | Paint the Hoop

For the mobile, you only need the inner ring of the embroidery hoop.
Brush on the yellow acrylic paint, completely covering all of the surfaces.
You may need to add a second coat.

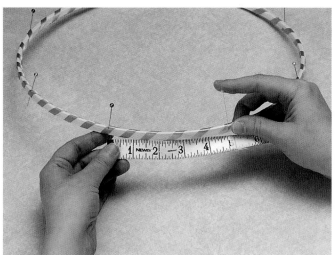

2 | Spiral Ribbon Around the Hoop

Use masking tape to secure the ribbon end onto the hoop, and then wrap
the ribbon counterclockwise around the hoop. Join the ribbon ends on the
inside of the hoop, overlapping them to make a continuous ribbon spiral.
Use craft glue to hold the ribbon in place. Remove the masking tape after
the glue has dried on the joined ribbons.

3 | Pin the Hoop at Equal Segments

Measure the hoop circumference and divide by eight. For a 12" (30cm)
hoop, each segment equals about 4⅞" (12cm). Mark each segment by
pinning vertically through the ribbon.

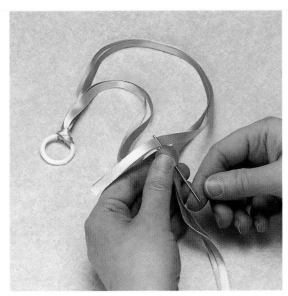

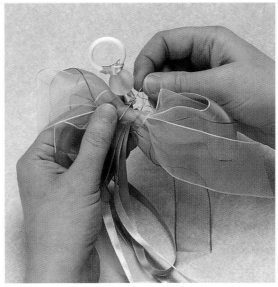

4 Loop the Ribbon and Thread the Bead

To make the harness for the mobile, cut two 14" (35cm) pieces of ¼" (7mm) wide ribbon—one pink and one blue. Place one ribbon directly on top of the other and fold them in half. Pass the fold through a plastic curtain ring, and then thread the ribbon tails through the loop. Pull it tightly. Thread the ribbon tails, two at a time, through the eye of a tapestry needle. Then pull them through the bead. Push the bead to the top of the harness. Knot all four ribbon strands together below the bead.

5 Add a Sheer Ribbon Bow

Lay the sheer blue ribbon on top of the sheer yellow ribbon. Treat them as one length of ribbon and tie them in a bow. Cut the ribbon tails at an angle, and seal them with glue to prevent unraveling. Sew the bow onto the ribbon harness, below the bead knot.

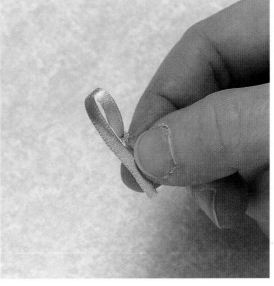

6 Attach the Harness

The carousel harness consists of four "arms" of ribbon. Sew the arms onto the hoop, spacing them equally apart (an arm at every other pin position). Alternate the ribbon colors, and make sure the ribbon doesn't twist. Wrap each ribbon end around the hoop as shown, then sew it in place at the corners with matching thread.

7 Add the Top Knot

Each paper bird is suspended from the mobile on a hanging strand of narrow ribbon. Cut two 10" (25cm) pieces each of pink, blue, lilac and yellow ⅛" (3mm) wide ribbon. Knot each piece of ribbon 2" (5cm) from an end. Loop the short section of ribbon down, behind the knot.

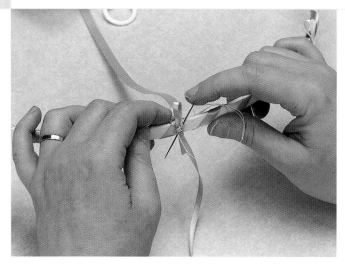

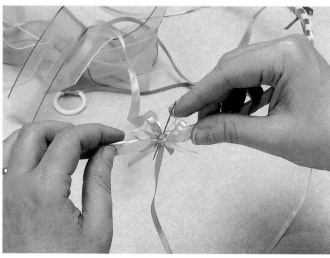

8 Sew Hanging Strands

Stitch the hanging strands onto the ribbon-wrapped hoop at the eight pinned positions. Sew through the knot, the loop of the hanging strand, and the spiralled ribbon, catching all layers. Use matching sewing thread. Alternate the ribbon colors—lilac, yellow, pink, blue—then repeat.

9 Tie a Mini-Bow

Sew a same-color bow, made from 8" (20cm) of $^1/_8$" (3mm) wide ribbon, onto each hanging strand, below the knot at the top. Seal the ends of each bow with glue to prevent unraveling.

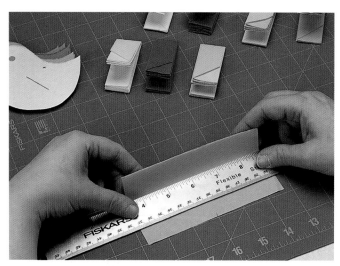

10 Begin Making the Chicks

Use the template provided to make eight chicks to hang from the carousel. For each chick, you need to glue two pieces of pearlescent paper back-to-back with a glue stick to make double-sided pieces of paper. Cut the wing slot and punch the small ribbon holes. Punch contrasting-colored dots, using the $^1/_4$" (7mm) circle punch, for the eyes. Glue the eyes in place using craft glue applied with a toothpick. For each pair of wings, cut a paper rectangle in a contrasting color measuring 8" x 5½" (20cm x 14cm). Make two pairs of wings in each paper color. Fold eight 1" (2.5cm) wide pleats across the width of each piece of paper, then fold the wings in half, creasing at the center.

11 Complete the Chicks

Make an angled cut at each wing end. Cut from the outer to the inner edge of the outside pleat. Slide the wings through the slot in each bird. Use a glue stick to fasten the wings onto each side. Tie a matching bow through the hole below the beak. Use 10" (25cm) of $^1/_8$" (3mm) wide ribbon for each bow. Stitch through the bow knot with matching thread to secure. To attach the chick knot the ribbon through the small punched hole at the top of each chick.

Many different versions of the carousel mobile are possible. Let your imagination take flight! Instead of paper chicks, substitute with origami animals, paper dolls, clip art cut-outs or minia-ture stuffed toys, to suggest a few.

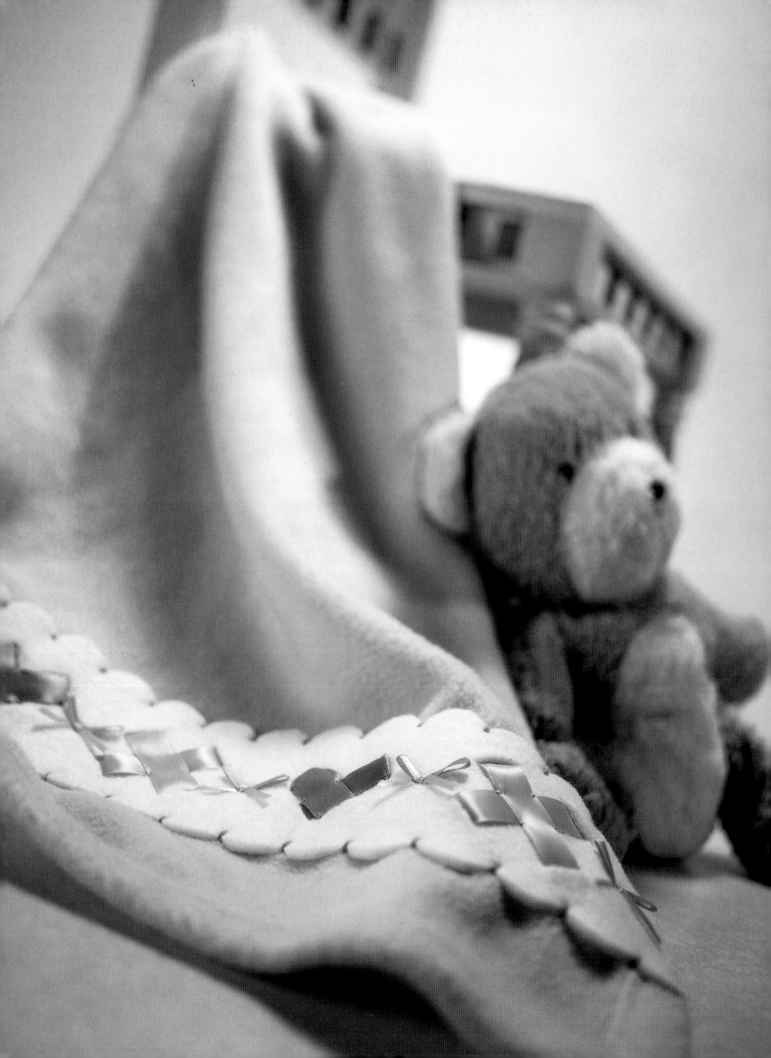

Love and Kisses Baby Blanket

What could be more cuddly than a baby wrapped

in a soft blanket? This project allows you to transform

a store-bought fleece blanket into a treasured baby

shower gift. And it doesn't take a long time to make!

To create the border design, strips of ribbon are

slipped into slits cut in the background fabric.

The precious baby will stay warm at night and feel

loved under this special keepsake.

Ribbon

- 1$\frac{1}{2}$ yards (1.3m) of $\frac{5}{8}$" (15mm) wide dusty pink single-face satin ribbon
- 1 yard (80cm) of $\frac{5}{8}$" (15mm) wide mint green single-face satin ribbon
- 4$\frac{1}{2}$ yards (4.1m) of $\frac{1}{8}$" (3mm) wide pink double-face satin ribbon

Supplies

- 28" (71cm) wide lilac acrylic fleece blanket
- $\frac{1}{2}$ yard (50cm) of white machine-washable felt
- $\frac{1}{2}$ yard (50cm) of fusible web
- $\frac{3}{8}$ yard (30cm) of fusible interfacing
- 1 skein each of mint green and dusty pink six-strand embroidery floss
- 1 skein of blue matte embroidery cotton
- craft knife and cutting mat
- embroidery, chenille and tapestry needles
- needle and thread
- straight pins
- fine-point pen or embroidery marker
- tape measure

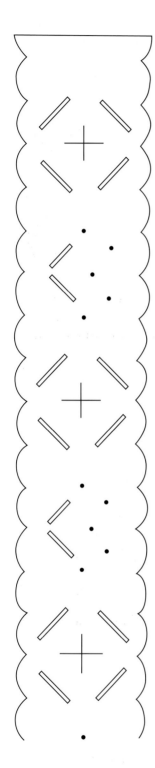

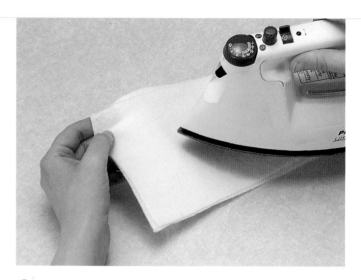

1 Fuse a Double Layer of Felt

Because you will be able to see the ribbon through the white felt, you need to double up the felt. For each of the two blanket borders, cut two strips, each measuring 4" (10cm) wide by the width of your baby blanket. Cut one strip of fusible web to the same dimensions for each of the two borders. Following the manufacturer's instructions, bond the two layers of each strip together. Prepare two borders in this way.

2 Stencil the Pattern Onto the Felt

Make a blanket border pattern in heavyweight paper using the template to the left. Cut out the slits with a craft knife. Pierce the dots with a tapestry needle. Pin the stencil onto the felt and mark the pattern through the slits and holes. (If you prefer not to use pen ink, use a special embroidery marker.) Cut the felt on the marked lines, using a craft knife pressed against a metal ruler. A good method is to make the initial cut with a craft knife, then use embroidery scissors to finish the job precisely. The pattern markings are on the wrong side of the border.

Use this template for the Love and Kisses Baby Blanket. Enlarge 143%.

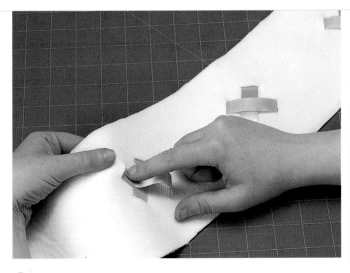

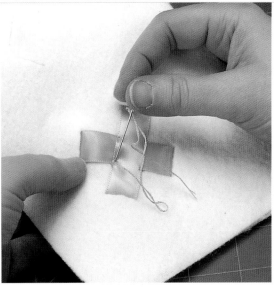

3 Insert the Ribbon "Kisses"

For each X-shaped "kiss," cut two 3¹/₄" (8cm) strips of ribbon. Insert the righthand side of the X into the slits first. Next, complete each X with the lefthand strip of ribbon.

4 Sew Down the Xs

To prevent little fingers from getting caught in the ribbon layers, sew down the corners. Thread a needle with two strands of embroidery floss, and take a few stitches at each ribbon corner.

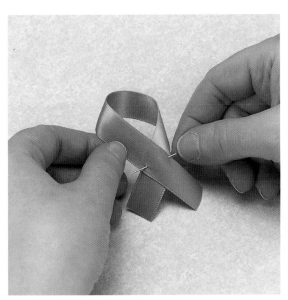

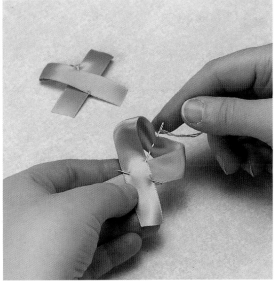

5 Make a Loop for the Heart

Pin a 6" (15cm) strip of ⁵/₈" (15mm) wide ribbon into a fish loop (see page 19), left ribbon over right, as shown. The tails extend ³/₄" (2cm) from the end.

6 Gather the Loop to Form the Heart

Thread a needle with a doubled strand of embroidery floss. Take three small stitches across the center top of the loop, then pull the gathers. With a stitch, connect the top of the loop to the intersection to form an X. Reinforce the shape with another stitch at the bottom of the intersecting ribbons. These shapes will become the hearts in the blanket.

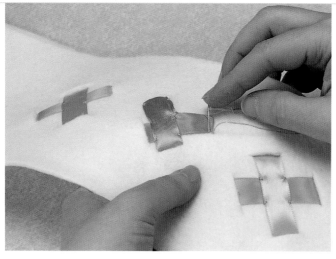

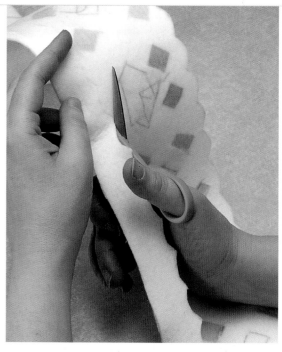

7 | Sew Hearts Onto the Border

Insert the tails into the slots, forming a heart. Pin the heart onto the felt (use the dots on the wrong side of the border as positioning guides for the top corners of the heart). Sew the heart onto the felt, making stitches at the corners and points where the ribbons cross.

8 | Iron Interfacing and Cut Scalloped Borders

Cut a piece of iron-on interfacing to the border dimensions. Iron it onto the wrong side of the border, following the manufacturer's instructions. This seals down all the ribbon ends. With embroidery scissors, cut scallops as marked along the top and bottom edges of the border.

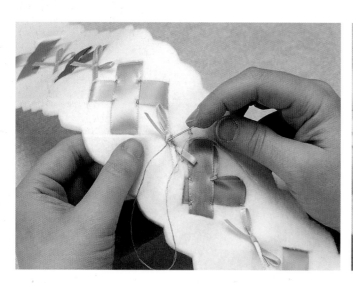

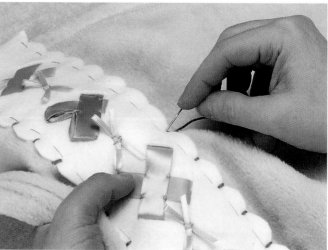

9 | Sew on the Accent Bows

For each bow, cut 8" (20cm) of narrow ribbon. Tie the bows and seal the ends of each bow. Sew a bow in between each heart and kiss. Stitch through the knot, so the bow cannot untie.

10 | Sew the Borders Onto the Blanket

Pin the borders onto the blanket, 3" (8cm) from the blanket edges. Baste the borders onto the blanket and remove any pins. Thread an embroidery needle with blue matte embroidery cotton, and sew the borders onto the blanket by stitching between the scallops.

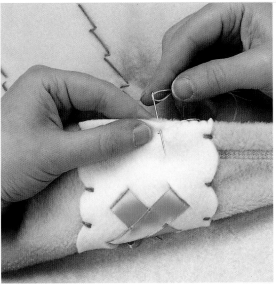

11 | Sew the Sides

For the baby's safety, stitch down the gaps at both sides of the borders. Thread a needle with white sewing thread and stitch the felt to the blanket.

variation idea

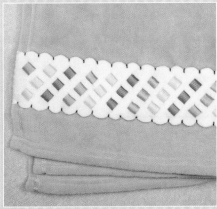

Ready for a more advanced slotted ribbon project? To make this multi-colored diamond-lattice border, insert diagonal bands of ribbon (⅝" [15mm] wide ribbon, each strip 4" [10cm] long, in three alternating colors) into the slotted felt background. The border is not difficult to make, but it does require patience.

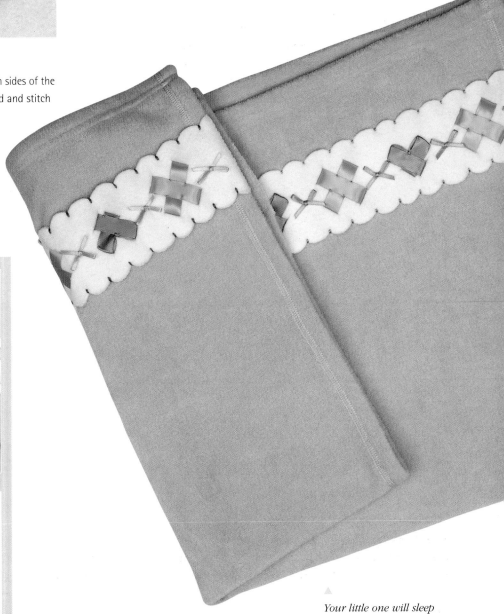

Your little one will sleep blissfully, wrapped in this Love and Kisses Blanket that you lovingly created.

✳ RIBBONS

BERISFORDS
P.O. Box 2
Thomas St.
Congelton
Cheshire CW12 1EF
United Kingdom
+44 (0) 1260
www.berisfords-ribbons.co.uk/contact.html
email: office@berisfords-ribbons.co.uk

• *Carrier of a variety of sheer and bridal ribbons*

C.M. OFFRAY & SONS, INC.
Lion Ribbon
Route 24
P.O. Box 601
Chester, NJ 07930-0601
(908) 879-4700
www.offray.com
email: questions@offray.com

• *Supplier of woven-edge satin, grosgrain and fancy ribbons*

CONSO PRODUCTS COMPANY
P.O. Box 326
513 N. Duncan By-pass
Union, SC 29379
1 (800) 845-2431
www.conso.com
email: info@conso.com

• *Distributor of decorative trims, cording, roping, tassels and fringes*

ELEGANT LACE
2960 Campbell Dr.
Auburn, CA 95602
1 (800) 623-6644
www.elegantlace.com
email: info@elegantlace .com

• *Carrier of hand dyed doilies for home décor, weddings, crafts, office and parties*

HOLLYWOOD TRIMS
Prym-Dritz USA
P.O. Box 5028
Spartanburg, SC 29304
www.dritz.com

• *Supplier of decorative braids, cords, fringes and tassels for fashion and home furniture*

HYMAN HENDLER AND SONS
67 W. Thirty-Eighth St.
New York, NY 10018
(212) 840-8393
www.hymanhendler.com
email: questions@hymanhendler.com

• *Distributor of a fabulous selection of ribbons*

LACIS
3162 Adeline St.
Berkeley, CA 94703
(510) 843-7178
www.lacis.com
email: staff@lacis.com

• *Supplier of lace and lace supplies, ribbons, tassels, stamens and beads*

M&J TRIMMINGS
1008 Sixth Ave.
New York, NY 10018
1 (800) 9-MJTRIM
www.mjtrim.com
email: mjtrim.info@mjtrim.com

• *Supplier of satin, grosgrain and taffeta ribbons*

RIBBON DESIGNS
P.O. Box 382
Edgware
Middlesex HA8 7XQ
United Kingdom
+44 (0) 20 8958
email: info@silkribbon.co.uk

• *International mail order supplier of ribbon, including satin, organdy and rat-tail cording*

THE RIBBON FACTORY
602 N. Brown St.
P.O. Box 405
Titusville, PA 16354
1 (866) 827-6431
www.ribbonfactory.com
email: ribbon@tbscc.com

• *Carrier of wired edge, grosgrain, lamé, satin, and decorative florals*

THE RIBBONERIE INC.
191 Potrero Ave.
San Francisco, CA 94103
(415) 626-6184
www.theribbonerie.com
email: theribbon@msn.com

• *Carrier of domestic and imported ribbons*

SELECTUS LIMITED
Panda Ribbons
The Uplands, Biddulph
Stoke-on-Trent, Staffs, England
ST8 7RH
United Kingdom
+44 (0) 1782 522316
www.selectus.co.uk
email: sales@selectus.co.uk

• *Seller of satins, taffeta, woven and printed fancies, tartens, metallics, velvets, bindings and galloons*

TINSEL TRADING COMPANY
47 W. Thirty-Eighth St.
New York, NY 10018
(212) 730-1030
www.tinseltrading.com
email: sales@tinseltrading.com

• *Distributor of antique trims, braids and ribbons*

YLI CORPORATION
161 W. Main St.
Rock Hill, SC 29730
(803) 985-3100
www.ylicorp.com
email: yli@ylicorp.com

• *Provider of pure silk ribbons, thread and yarn*

✳ CRAFTS
- -

BROOKLACE, INC.
300 Callegari Dr.
West Haven, CT 06516
(203) 937-4555
www.brooklace.com
email: info@brooklace.com

• *Manufacturer of lace and linen doilies in a variety of shapes and sizes*

DALEE BOOK CO.
129 Clinton Pl.
Yonkers, NY 10701
(914) 965-1660
1 (800) 852-2665
www.daleebook.com

• *Manufacturer of archival-quality, acid-free bridal albums and scrapbooks*

FISKARS BRANDS, INC.
7811 W. Stewart Ave.
Wausau, WI 54401
(715) 842-2091
1 (800) 950-0203
www.fiskars.com

• *Manufacturer of scissors, paper edgers and hand punches*

FRED ALDOUS LTD.
37 Lever St.
Manchester M1 1LW
Lancs
United Kingdom
08707 517 300
www.fredaldous.co.uk
email: aldous@btinternet.com

• *Mail-order craft supplier of crafts, including papier maché boxes*

KUNIN FELT
Foss Manufacturing Company
380 Lafayette Rd.
P.O. Box 5000
Hampton, NH 03843-5000
(603) 929-6100
www.kuninfelt.com
email: kuninfelt@fossmfg.com

• *Manufacturer of machine-washable Rainbow Classic felt*

PHRAZZLE CARD
Phrazzle House
29 Hest View Rd.
Ulverston
Cumbria LA12 9PH
United Kingdom
01229 588880
www.phrazzlecard.co.uk
email: phrazzle@nessaby.co.uk

• *Mail order supplier of corrugated cardboard and pearlescent paper*

Get creative with North Light Books!

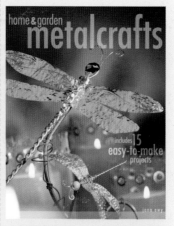

CREATE YOUR own luxurious bars of soap today—the kind that lather, clean and smell better than store-bought—and start babying your skin tonight. Simply combine ingredients, cook as directed, add fragrances, place in molds and voila! Using equipment as easy as your oven or crock pot, you've made soap that'll be ready to use in an hour!

ISBN 1-58180-268-4, paperback, 128 pages, #32138-K

YOU CAN make your own tabletop fountains and add beautiful accents to your living room, bedroom, kitchen and garden. These 15 gorgeous step-by-step projects make it easy, using everything from lava rock and bamboo to shells and clay pots. You'll learn to incorporate flowers, driftwood, fire, figurines, crystals, plants and more.

ISBN 1-58180-103-3, paperback, 128 pages, #31791-K

YOU CAN create gorgeous home decor and garden art using today's new, craft-friendly metals, meshes and wire. You'll find 15 projects inside, ranging from lamps to picture frames. Most can be completed in an afternoon! You'll learn how to texture, antique and emboss your work, then embellish it with glass beads, scented candles, colorful ribbons and more.

ISBN 1-58180-330-3, paperback, 96 pages, #32296-K

THESE 20 beautiful wreath projects are perfect for celebrating those special times of year. You'll find a range of sizes and styles, utilizing a variety of creative materials, including dried herbs, cinnamon sticks, silk flowers, Autumn leaves, Christmas candy and more. Clear, step-by-step instructions ensure beautiful, long lasting results every time!

ISBN 1-58180-239-0, paperback, 144 pages, #32015-K

These books and other fine North Light titles are available from your local art & craft retailer, bookstore, online supplier or by calling 1-800-448-0915.